Joe Hisaishi's Soundtrack for My Neighbor Totoro

33 1/3 Global

33 1/3 Global, a series related to but independent from **33 1/3**, takes the format of the original series of short, music-based books and brings the focus to music throughout the world. With initial volumes focusing on Japanese and Brazilian music, the series will also include volumes on the popular music of Australia/Oceania, Europe, Africa, the Middle East, and more.

33 1/3 Japan

Series Editor: Noriko Manabe

Spanning a range of artists and genres—from the 1970s rock of Happy End to technopop band Yellow Magic Orchestra, the Shibuya-kei of Cornelius, classic anime series *Cowboy Bebop*, J-Pop/EDM hybrid Perfume, and vocaloid star Hatsune Miku—**33 1/3 Japan** is a series devoted to in-depth examination of Japanese popular music of the twentieth and twenty-first centuries.

Published Titles:
Supercell's *Supercell* by Keisuke Yamada
Yoko Kanno's *Cowboy Bebop Soundtrack* by Rose Bridges
Perfume's *Game* by Patrick St. Michel
AKB48 by Patrick W. Galbraith & Jason G. Karlin
Cornelius's *Fantasma* by Martin Roberts
Joe Hisaishi's *Soundtrack for My Neighbor Totoro* by Kunio Hara

Forthcoming titles:
Nenes' *Koza Dabasa* by Henry Johnson
Shonen Knife's *Happy Hour* by Brooke McCorkle

33 1/3 Brazil

Series Editor: Jason Stanyek

Covering the genres of samba, tropicália, rock, hip hop, forró, bossa nova, heavy metal and funk, among others, **33 1/3 Brazil** is a series devoted to in-depth examination of the most important Brazilian albums of the twentieth and twenty-first centuries.

Published Titles:

Caetano Veloso's *A Foreign Sound* by Barbara Browning
Tim Maia's *Tim Maia Racional Vols. 1 &2* by Allen Thayer
João Gilberto and Stan Getz's *Getz/Gilberto* by Brian McCann
Dona Ivone Lara's *Sorriso Negro* by Mila Burns
Gilberto Gil's *Refazenda* by Marc A. Hertzman

Forthcoming titles:

Milton Nascimento and Lô Borges's *The Corner Club* by
    Jonathon Grasse
Racionais MCs' *Sobrevivendo no Inferno* by Marília Gessa and
    Derek Pardue
Jorge Ben Jor's *África Brasil* by Frederick J. Moehn
Naná Vasconcelos's *Saudades* by Daniel B. Sharp

33 1/3 Europe

Series Editor: Fabian Holt

Spanning a range of artists and genres, **33 1/3 Europe** offers engaging accounts of popular and culturally significant albums of Continental Europe and the North Atlantic from the twentieth and twenty first centuries.

Forthcoming Titles:

Modeselektor's *Happy Birthday* by Sean Nye
Heiner Müller and Heiner Goebbels's *Wolokolamsker Chaussee* by
    Philip V. Bohlman
Ivo Papasov's *Balkanology* by Carol Silverman
Darkthrone's *A Blaze in the Northern Sky* by Ross Hagen

Joe Hisaishi's Soundtrack for My Neighbor Totoro

Kunio Hara

Noriko Manabe, Series Editor

BLOOMSBURY ACADEMIC
NEW YORK • LONDON • OXFORD • NEW DELHI • SYDNEY

BLOOMSBURY ACADEMIC
Bloomsbury Publishing Inc
1385 Broadway, New York, NY 10018, USA
50 Bedford Square, London, WC1B 3DP, UK

BLOOMSBURY, BLOOMSBURY ACADEMIC and the Diana logo are
trademarks of Bloomsbury Publishing Plc

First published in the United States of America 2020

For legal purposes the Acknowledgments on p. xiv constitute an
extension of this copyright page.

Cover design: Louise Dugdale
Cover image: *My Neighbor Totoro*, 1988. © 50th Street Films /
Courtesy Everett Collection / Mary Evans

Bloomsbury Publishing Inc does not have any control over, or
responsibility for, any third-party websites referred to or in this book. All
internet addresses given in this book were correct at the time of going
to press. The author and publisher regret any inconvenience caused if
addresses have changed or sites have ceased to exist, but can accept no
responsibility for any such changes.

Library of Congress Cataloging-in-Publication Data
Names: Hara, Kunio, author.
Title: Joe Hisaishi's Soundtrack for My Neighbor Totoro / Kunio Hara.
Description: [1.] | New York: Bloomsbury Academic, 2020. |
Series: 33 1/3 Japan | Includes bibliographical references and index. |
Summary: "Miyazaki Hayao's beloved animated film, My Neighbor
Totoro (1988), expresses nostalgia for both an innocent past and a
distant home, sentiments greatly enhanced by Joe Hisaishi's music"–
Provided by publisher.
Identifiers: LCCN 2019034907 (print) | LCCN 2019034908 (ebook) |
ISBN 9781501345128 (paperback) | ISBN 9781501345111 (hardback) |
ISBN 9781501345135 (epub) | ISBN 9781501345142 (pdf)
Subjects: LCSH: Hisaishi, Jō, 1950-. Tonari no Totoro. | Tonari no Totoro
(Motion picture) | Animated film music–Japan–History and criticism.
Classification: LCC ML410.H688 H37 2020 (print) | LCC ML410.H688
(ebook) | DDC 781.5/42–dc23
LC record available at https://lccn.loc.gov/2019034907
LC ebook record available at https://lccn.loc.gov/2019034908

ISBN: HB: 978-1-5013-4511-1
PB: 978-1-5013-4512-8
ePDF: 978-1-5013-4514-2
eBook: 978-1-5013-4513-5

Series: 33 1/3 Japan

Typeset by Deanta Global Publishing Services, Chennai, India
Printed and bound in the United States of America

For Mom and Dad

Contents

Examples

Preface

Throughout this book, I refer to Japanese names following the traditional order, with the last name followed by the first name: for example, Miyazaki Hayao. One exception is Joe Hisaishi who has an active international career as a composer, performer, and conductor. When referring to Japanese scholars whose published works include both Japanese and English, I use the name orders as they appear in the published documents.

When referring to publications in Japanese in the text, I use the English translation followed by the Romanized title at first mention for ease of reading. Several Japanese secondary sources I cite in this document are also available in English translations. Many essays by Miyazaki, Hisaishi, and others that have appeared in magazines and newspapers, were later collected and reprinted as books. Whenever possible, I tried to consult the original documents and compared them with later reprints.

When referring to the titles of composition on the image song album and the soundtrack album for *My Neighbor Totoro*, I use their English translations followed by Romanized titles and track numbers at first mention. The track numbers are preceded by "I" when they are included on the image song album and "S" when they are included on the soundtrack album. I use these labels to eliminate any confusion when multiple tracks share the same titles.

The original 1987 LP of *My Neighbor Totoro: Image Song Collection* by Animage Records included lead sheets of the songs with their lyrics. In 2018, Studio Ghibli Records released a reprint of this LP, complete with liner notes and lead sheets. Unless otherwise noted, measure numbers included in the musical analyses in this book refer to these lead sheets. Additionally, the text provides timestamps (in minutes and seconds) for key moments in the music, in parentheses (MM:SS) for recorded versions of songs. Timestamps (in hours, minutes, and seconds) for scenes from the film are provided in square brackets [H:MM:SS] based on the 2010 Disney DVD release of the work.

In order to create the musical examples in this book, I first studied the albums and the film soundtrack, then consulted the lead sheets included in the reprint of the LP of *My Neighbor Totoro: Image Song Collection,* as well as *Piano Collection: "My Neighbor Totoro"* (2014), a collection of solo piano arrangements, published by kmp, of pieces from the image and soundtrack albums.

Acknowledgments

I would like to thank my mentors, colleagues, students, family, and friends who have encouraged and supported me throughout the process of writing this book. I am especially grateful to Noriko Manabe, the series editor of 33 1/3 Japan, for her musical as well as critical insights and her guidance. I would also like to thank Leah Babb-Rosenfeld, the senior editor at Bloomsbury, for giving me the opportunity to write about the music of this delightful film. Anonymous reviewers have given me valuable comments and suggestions, which have helped me refine my ideas. I thank them for sharing their expertise with me. Thank you also to Brooke McCorkle for her willingness to listen to my ideas and her encouragement to write.

Many people, colleagues, friends, and students, have shared with me their love for the film and expressed genuine enthusiasm and excitement for this project. Their stories have inspired me to think deeply about the impact of Hisaishi's music in the way we experience Miyazaki's *My Neighbor Totoro*. Thank you to my family in Japan, who helped me gather books and music related to the film and arranged outings to the Ghibli Museum in Tokyo and Satsuki and Mei's House near Nagoya. Thank you also to my family in Kentucky who have given me continuous encouragement throughout the process. Finally, a big, Totoro-sized thank you to my husband, Danny Jenkins, for all that he has done for me to help me write this book.

Introduction

Totoro! The name alone brings smiles to the faces of people who have seen Miyazaki Hayao's beloved 1988 animated film, *My Neighbor Totoro* (*Tonari no Totoro*). To me, the name Totoro conjures up the image of a large, furry, owl-shaped creature with stubby limbs, long claws, tall pointy ears, small eyes, and a wide flat snout, wearing an enormous grin. It also inspires a sense of comfort and warmth, joy and happiness, even on days I don't otherwise feel too upbeat. The large variety of merchandise bearing the image of Totoro found in Japan today suggests the enduring popularity of Miyazaki's film over the past three decades. Increasingly, these items can be found in the United States (where I live now) at Japanese bookstores, specialty stores catering to the fans of anime, some mainstream big-box stores, and, of course, online retailers. I frequently hear from friends and colleagues about how much they and their young children love the film, or meet students at my university who have grown up watching it. To these fans of the movie, I suspect that the name Totoro also brings a warm and fuzzy feeling that makes them smile.

There is, however, another common reaction to hearing the name Totoro I observed among the people I've encountered: singing. When I strike up a conversation about Totoro with someone familiar with the film, inevitably one or both of us end up singing the catchy hook from the film's theme song, "My Neighbor Totoro," composed by Joe Hisaishi. Indeed, under certain circumstances, we might go on singing, "To'toro To' *to*-ro To' toro To' *to*-ro" for a long time, blissfully chanting this simple but handsomely crafted tune as if it were a famous nursery rhyme. Helen McCarthy recounts overhearing a young boy singing the tune as they crossed each other on a road in Shinjuku, the incredibly busy administrative hub in Tokyo (McCarthy 1999, 135). I once witnessed a family of perfect strangers start to sing the song in a grocery store parking lot when they saw a decal of Totoro I had on the back windshield of my car in Columbia, South Carolina, on the other side of the globe.

It is not uncommon for an animated film to have a strong musical association—just think of the song, "Let It Go" by Kristen Anderson-Lopez and Robert Lopez, which became synonymous with Walt Disney's mega-hit *Frozen* (2013). However, unlike *Frozen* or many other Disney animated features, such as *The Little Mermaid* (1988), *Beauty and the Beast* (1991), and *Aladdin* (1992) to list a few films produced around the same time, *My Neighbor Totoro* was not conceived as a musical. As such, unlike in Disney films, the theme song is never sung by a character within the narrative of the animation. Although the melody derived from the song appears elsewhere in the film, the sung rendition of "My Neighbor Totoro" only comes at the very end of the film, underscoring the final wordless montage sequence and the end credits.

In spite of the relatively minor role that it plays in the film itself, the song "My Neighbor Totoro" functions as a sonic icon of the film, *My Neighbor Totoro*, attesting to the special role that

Hisaishi's music plays in Miyazaki's film. But why, then, does Hisaishi's music, particularly this theme song, so profoundly color the way we think about the film? Does it have to do with the way that the two creative artists, Miyazaki and Hisaishi, collaborated to create their final product? What exactly was the process of their collaboration like, and how extensively did they work on this project together? What else can we learn about the film by focusing our attention on the music associated with the film? In this book, I try to answer these and other related questions about the role of Hisaishi's music in Miyazaki's film, *My Neighbor Totoro*.

Nostalgia in *My Neighbor Totoro*

Set in a fictional village somewhere west of Tokyo, *My Neighbor Totoro* follows the adventures, both mundane and fantastical, of two young sisters, Satsuki (in the fourth grade, that is, aged nine or ten years) and Mei (four years old) in the summer of 1957 (more often referred to as sometime in the Shōwa 30s, or 1955–1964). The film opens with the sisters moving into their new home with their father, an archaeologist who works at a university in Tokyo. Later, we learn that Satsuki and Mei's mother is in a nearby hospital, recovering from an unspecified illness. The sisters also encounter strange creatures, both inside the house and outside in the backyard, facing a tall camphor tree at the top of a small hill. One day, by accident, Mei discovers the trio of creatures she calls "totoro"—fuzzy, round, imaginary beings with pointy ears and stubby limbs that come in three sizes: small, medium, and large. As the film unfolds, it becomes apparent that despite their outward expression of contentment and joy, both sisters suffer deeply from the pain of being separated from their mother, as well as the occasional reminder that they may lose her forever. Nevertheless, with the help of their father, their friends, caring adults, and forest creatures, the sisters overcome their struggles with admirable pluck and verve.

In discussing the relationship between Hisaishi's music and Miyazaki's film, I focus on the concept of nostalgia. The word nostalgia itself has a long and complicated history dating back to the late eighteenth century, when a medical student in Switzerland coined the word to describe a fatal form of illness known locally as *Heimweh* or homesickness by combining two Greek words, *nostos* (return to the native land) and *algos* (suffering or grief) (Starobinski 1966, 85). Over the following centuries, the meaning of the word changed gradually to denote a feeling, "a positively toned evocation of the lived past" according to Fred Davis (1979, 18), rather than illness. Marilyn Ivy's (1995, 10) fascinating study of Japanese culture at the end of the twentieth century—the exact point in history when *My Neighbor Totoro* came into being—posits nostalgia, defined here as "an ambivalent longing to erase the temporal difference between subject and object of desire," as a productive, guiding emotion of the era. Likewise, numerous commentators have argued eloquently and convincingly about the centrality of nostalgia in *My Neighbor Totoro* (Swale 2015; Napier 2018).

Indeed, images of bucolic landscapes and depictions of now partially forgotten daily and seasonal routines of people living in a rural Japanese community from the recent past suffuse the film. Somewhat surprisingly, however, very few critics and viewers have commented on the ability of Hisaishi's music to arouse a similar sentiment of yearning for the past.[1] Music has historically been understood to function as a powerful trigger for nostalgia (Davis 1979; Yano 2002; Hughes 2008; Wilson 2014), as witnessed in countless commercials, TV dramas, and films. Yet, unlike the visual components of the film, Hisaishi's score for Miyazaki's *My Neighbor Totoro* lacks conventional cues, such as "oldies" playing on the radio, designed to arouse feelings of nostalgia in its viewers. Instead, I argue that Hisaishi's music interacts with the concept of nostalgia at a more abstract level. Hisaishi's music highlights, enhances, and invites us to feel the intensely felt longing for a permanent and stable home that the protagonists of the film experience. It helps us to recall happier moments in our own past and to look toward a brighter future.

Reading through Miyazaki's writings and interviews about *My Neighbor Totoro*, one bumps into a glaring challenge to the premise of the argument outlined above: Miyazaki adamantly claims that he did not make the film for nostalgia. For instance, in his "Project Plan for *My Neighbor Totoro*," dated December 1, 1986, Miyazaki (2009, 255) stresses that the film "needs to be a lively and fresh piece of entertainment, not full of reminiscence [*kaiko*] and nostalgia [*kyōshū*]." Miyazaki (1988, 122–39) takes a similar position in an extended interview with the Japanese writer Ikeda Noriaki, originally published in *Ghibli Roman Album: "My Neighbor Totoro,"* entitled, "*Totoro* Is Not a Work Made from Nostalgia [*natsukashisa*]" (Totoro wa natsukashisa kara tsukutta sakuhinja naindesu).[2] In a different conversation with Itoi Shigesato originally published in 1990, Miyazaki

(1996, 368) complains about the reputation of *My Neighbor Totoro* as a nostalgic film. He even confesses that "I get mad the most when people tell me that it's nostalgic [*natsukashii*]." In his comprehensive guide to Miyazaki's films, Kanō Seiji (2006, 129) paraphrases these statements and concludes that "Miyazaki emphasized multiple times that 'this work was not made because of nostalgia [*nosutaruji*].'" Nevertheless, the statement demonstrates that, whether Miyazaki likes it or not, *My Neighbor Totoro* does elicit nostalgic reactions among its viewers.

To probe more deeply into this conundrum, I would like to take a closer look at the conversation with Itoi mentioned above. After declaring his annoyance with nostalgia, Miyazaki (1996, 369) describes a curious interaction he had with his child about a polluted river near their house. When Miyazaki told his son that the river had been clean until about ten years earlier, his son suddenly became very angry. Reflecting on this incident, Miyazaki interpreted his son's anger as an indictment against him and other adults who are unable or unwilling to do anything about the problem they acknowledge. What connects Miyazaki's dislike of nostalgia and this recollection, I believe, is his resistance toward the allure of nostalgia to celebrate the past that depends upon the devaluation of the conditions in the present. In this temporal framework, children who do not have any personal memory of the past are predetermined to become merely the objects of pity and melancholic reflection for the adults. Furthermore, these adults are often themselves responsible for the very deplorable conditions they mourn for their children. In sum, Miyazaki understands *natsukashisa* as a self-indulgent and unproductive sentiment intended for adults to wallow in their fond memories of the past and nothing more.

Nevertheless, Miyazaki's apparent resistance to nostalgia points to another crucial nature of the concept––its ability to function as a rhetorical device that carries a potent political message. Literary critic Stuart Tannock (1995, 454) recognizes nostalgia as a "cultural resource or strategy" that enables actors to construct an argument pitting the past against the present. In this model, the present is always understood to be lacking in some ways. The desire to correct this deficiency, Tannock observes, can motivate groups of people to organize and act in certain ways to restore the conditions from the past. As such, nostalgia can be a powerful sentiment that undergirds reactionary ideologies that aim to reinstate oppressive political, social, cultural conditions or dupe people into longing for the "good old days" that never actually existed. Anthropologist Jennifer Robertson (1988) demonstrates that starting in the 1970s, Japanese politicians, government officials, city planners, and citizens engaged in a similar discourse around the idea of *furusato*, a Japanese word denoting "old village," or more precisely a person's "hometown," drawing on nostalgia's powerful rhetorical appeal.[3] Nostalgic discussion about *furusato*, an idealized reimagining of rural village communities as something superior to the living conditions in the impersonal urban centers, was therefore commonplace in Japan at the time Miyazaki produced his films. In recent years, Miyazaki has openly espoused an oppositional position to the conservative Liberal Democratic Party (LDP) government's goal of restoring "normalcy" by revising Article 9 of the postwar constitution (Napier 2018, 3).[4] Miyazaki's rejections of nostalgia in *My Neighbor Totoro* can also be understood, perhaps, as an effort to dissociate himself from this conservative political discourse. Indeed, although *My Neighbor Totoro* takes place in the Japanese countryside of the recent past, the village community rarely takes center stage. In fact, Miyazaki appears to emphasize the distance of Satsuki and Mei, outsiders from the urban center, from the villagers and their lack of connection to the land they inhabit.[5]

Although nostalgia in most political contexts often carries a negative and at times dangerous connotation, Tannock reminds us that progressive causes often use nostalgia for their political ends as well. Nostalgia can, for instance, provide a way to seek out positive models in the past to solve the problems in the present, leading to a more utopic state. For those who live on the margins of society, retreating into history and remembering better conditions from the past may be the only way to survive the truly deplorable conditions in the present moment. Tannock calls this move "retrieval" in his essay:

> This return to the past to read a historical continuity of struggle, identity, and community, this determination to comb the past for every sense of possibility and destiny it might contain—digging around central structures to find the breathing-spaces of the margins, spinning up old sources into tales of gargantuan epic—is a resource and strategy central to the struggles of all subaltern cultural and social groups. Nostalgia here works to retrieve the past for the support in building the future. (1995, 129)

In other words, nostalgia has the potential to become a positive, generative force that goes beyond the longing reflection of the irrevocable past.

As it turns out, Miyazaki had written one of his first essays about animation that highlights this very aspect of nostalgia. In an early essay titled "Nostalgia for a Lost World," published in the March 1979 issue of the Japanese magazine *Animēshon*, Miyazaki (1996, 43) identifies nostalgia (*kyōshū*) as the driving force behind those who create anime as well as the "middle-teens" who consume it.[6] Although he initially presents the widely accepted definition of nostalgia as a "word used to describe the longings adults experience for their childhood," Miyazaki points out that even three- and five-year-old children share similar sentiments. This sentiment, he explains, is the keenly felt "longing for a lost world" (43). According to Miyazaki, at the very moment a person enters the world and becomes locked into a specific time and place in history, they lose their possibility to exist in another time and place. This accident of birth, in turn, plants in their mind an impossible longing for access to a world to which they do not belong. Miyazaki claims that by creating opportunities for the creators and viewers to inhabit imaginary landscapes and worlds, anime functions as a "substitution" (*daiyōhin*) to satisfy this longing (44).

In writing about *My Neighbor Totoro*, Miyazaki clearly engages with the idea of nostalgia in this sense—as a creative impetus to show a world that is not accessible to viewers. In the "Project Plan," Miyazaki (1996, 397–98) outlines his desire to "create a film that makes lovers even more fond of each other, parents reminisce fondly about their childhood, and children explore the backside of Shinto shrines or climb up a tree in hopes of meeting Totoro." Miyazaki (1988, 125) elaborates on this point in the interview, reiterating his wishful thoughts that "after seeing this film, children might go running in the fields, pick up acorns, play behind the shrines (although there are very few places remaining like that), or feel excited at having peeked under the crawlspace of their own houses." By showing a version of the past, augmented with fantastical creatures from his own imagination, Miyazaki hoped that the children of his day would find something useful from the past.

A careful reading of Miyazaki's comments about nostalgia and the film thus reveals that he has attributed a narrowly circumscribed definition to the concept of nostalgia as an exclusionary sentiment. Yet, for children to be motivated to explore nature surrounding them, they first have to feel the desire, the longing to recuperate somehow the world depicted in the film. While those suffering from nostalgia cannot reverse time, they are able to visit the place to which they long to return. Children who watch *My Neighbor Totoro*, likewise, cannot reverse history. However, they are still able to visit the Japanese countryside. And if the countryside no longer looks like the way it is depicted in the film, they can work toward restoring it to its former state. As Chihiro, the protagonist from another film by Miyazaki, *Spirited Away* (*Sen to Chihiro no kamikakushi*, 2001), demonstrates, today's children can still restore the dirty river to a clean stream without giving up. In this way, nostalgia can become a roadmap for a brighter future. The question, then, is: What does this nostalgia sound like in *My Neighbor Totoro*?

* * *

Writing this book has made me think back to the late 1980s, when Miyazaki's *My Neighbor Totoro* was released in Japan, and the music I listened to then. A fan of Hisaishi's music and Miyazaki's films, I had collected CDs of *Nausicaä of the Valley of* the Wind (*Kaze no tani no Naushika*, 1984) and *Castle in the Sky* (*Tenkū no shiro Rapyuta*, 1986) but had not yet purchased the CDs of *My Neighbor Totoro*. Recently, my mother gave back to me a binder of sheet music from my middle school band that she had been keeping all these years. It contained a little surprise: a tattered copy of the tuba part to the film's theme song, "My Neighbor Totoro." Even though I had not actively sought out the CDs of the film, its music, especially its two theme songs, had been lodged in my mind. Like the differently shaped acorns that Satsuki and Mei plant in the garden and which grow into one big tree, the diverse songs and instrumental music that Hisaishi composed are buried deep in my memory; from time to time, they rise up to the surface of my consciousness, creating an awesome sonic impression of *My Neighbor Totoro*.

Unquestionably, *My Neighbor Totoro* is a long-standing international icon of Japanese pop culture, produced by two of the most prominent and widely celebrated Japanese artists in recent decades, Miyazaki Hayao and Joe Hisaishi. Beloved the world over, the film is well known to many. By engaging with a lesser known musical source—Hisaishi's *Image Song Collection*—and texts that are yet to be translated into English, this book aims to give readers a fresh look at this anime classic, focusing on the nostalgic effects of the sonic material itself, as well as the audience's experiences with it. For those new to the film, this book presents a take on how this world-famous animator, Miyazaki, collaborated closely with one of today's most prolific and famous film composers, Hisaishi, on *My Neighbor Totoro*. For fans of the film, the book is an invitation to reacquaint themselves with *My Neighbor Totoro* through a deep dive into the film's music—bright and cheerful but, at times, also wistful and melancholic.

1 Miyazaki, Hisaishi, and Their Collaboration

When *My Neighbor Totoro* was released in movie theaters in Japan on April 16, 1988, Miyazaki was a 47-year-old veteran of the Japanese animation industry.[1] It was the fourth feature-length animation that he directed, and his third film with Hisaishi,[2] with whom he has collaborated since *Nausicaä of the Valley of the Wind* (1984) through his most recent full-length film, *The Wind Rises* (*Kaze tachinu*, 2013). A brief discussion of their respective careers up to *My Neighbor Totoro,* as well as the nature and process of their collaboration, provides a background for understanding the music for the film.

Miyazaki Hayao: A Biographical Sketch

Miyazaki became interested in animation after watching *The Tale of the White Serpent* (*Hakujaden*, 1958), Tōei Animation's first feature-length color animation, when he was eighteen and cramming for the college entrance exam (Miyazaki 1996, 44). In 1959, Miyazaki entered the political economy department at Gakushūin University. He had wanted to join a student manga club (circle) but was unable to find one and, instead, joined a club that studied children's literature. This experience provided him with the opportunity to familiarize himself with a new breed of Japanese children's literature, including the works of Nakagawa Rieko. After graduating from college in 1963, he joined Tōei Animation, where he spent the next seven years working as an animator. There, he met Takahata Isao, with whom he would collaborate over the next few decades. In 1971, Miyazaki quit Tōei Animation and joined another animation studio, A Production, with Takahata. He collaborated with Takahata on the TV anime series *Lupin III* (*Rupan sansei*, 1971–72) and two medium-length theatrical anime, *Panda! Go, Panda!* (*Panda kopanda*, 1972) and its sequel, *Panda! Go, Panda!: The Rainy-Day Circus* (*Panda kopanda amefuri sākasu*, 1973). Miyazaki and Takahata made another move in 1973 to Zuiyō Eizō (which later reorganized itself as Nippon Animation), where Miyazaki participated in several notable TV series based on well-known children's literature, including *Heidi, Girl of the Alps* (*Arupusu no shōjo Haiji*, 1974), *A Dog of Flanders* (*Furandāsu no inu*, 1975), *3,000 Leagues in Search of Mother* (*Haha o tazunete sanzenri*, 1976), *Rascal the Raccoon* (*Araiguma Rasukaru*, 1978), and *Anne of Green Gables* (*Akage no An*, 1979). It is significant to note that many of these series center on the lives of children, especially young girls, in realistic Western settings.

After Miyazaki had fulfilled many supportive functions as an animator in the 1960s and 1970s, he began to take on leadership roles starting in the late 1970s. Miyazaki made his directorial debut with the TV series, *Future Boy Conan* (*Miraishōnen Konan*, 1978), a postapocalyptic sci-fi fantasy based on American author Alexander Key's *The Incredible Tide* (1970). This was quickly followed by *The Castle of Cagliostro* (*Kariosutoro no shiro*, 1979), a comedy-action drama film featuring characters from the popular *Lupin III* manga by Monkey Punch. This was the first feature-length animation that Miyazaki directed. In 1982, Miyazaki started the serial publication of his own postapocalyptic sci-fi fantasy manga, *Nausicaä of the Valley of the Wind,* in the magazine *Animage* published by Tokuma Shoten, initiating a long association with the publisher. The following year, Miyazaki started working on the animated film version of *Nausicaä* as its director with the animation studio Topcraft. The success of the film, which was released in 1984, encouraged Miyazaki and Takahata (who had managed the film as its producer) to found their own animation company, Studio Ghibli, in 1985 with an investment from Tokuma Shoten. Studio Ghibli released its very first film— *Castle in the Sky*, a steampunk[3] adventure film inspired, in part, by Jonathan Swift's *Gulliver's Travels*—in August 1986.

The list of films directed by Miyazaki suggests his preference for fantasy and adventure films intended for teenagers and young adults. *Totoro*, which follows the ordinary (and at times extraordinary) daily activities of a pair of young sisters, marked a radical departure from the reputation that Miyazaki had forged up to this point. His earlier works, especially at Nippon Animation with Takahata, demonstrate his familiarity with narratives centering on young children (Greenberg 2018, 117). Yet, the setting of *Totoro*—the Japanese countryside rather than a foreign locale—also signaled an important shift in priorities (Napier 2018, 104). In fact, this was the first of Miyazaki's many films set in Japan, which include *Princess*

Mononoke (*Mononoke hime*, 1997), Spirited Away (2001), *Ponyo* (*Gake no ue no Ponyo*, 2008), and *The Wind Rises* (2013).

In spite of this apparent anomaly, *My Neighbor Totoro* represented for Miyazaki a culmination of ideas he had nurtured over several decades. Twice before the late 1980s, Miyazaki had attempted to launch similar projects. In 1975, during the transitionary period between his work on *Heidi* and *3,000 Leagues*, Miyazaki produced two sketches, called "image boards" (*imēji bōdo*), depicting scenes of a small girl interacting with a mysterious monster at the bus stop on a rainy evening. These and other sketches are reproduced in *The Place Where Totoro Was Born* (*Totoro no umareta tokoro*) (Miyazaki 2018, 2–3). The first sketch shows a girl, holding an umbrella at a bus stop at night, spotting a dark yeti-like creature approaching her, with only its eyes visible, covering its head with a huge green leaf. The second image shows this monster on a cat-shaped bus handing a little sack to the girl. These were initially prepared for a planned children's picture book, but the project never came to fruition. After completing *The Castle of Cagliostro*, Miyazaki revisited the idea and produced additional sketches, but this attempt, too, did not materialize. As the work for *Castle in the Sky* approached its end, Miyazaki began to ponder taking on the project in earnest. However, the executives of Studio Ghibli's parent company, Tokuma Shoten, expressed concerns about the commercial viability of the film. The situation changed once Suzuki Toshio, the assistant editor of *Animage*, negotiated a deal—unprecedented in the industry—for Studio Ghibli to produce simultaneously *My Neighbor Totoro* and *Grave of the Fireflies* (*Hotaru no haka*) on behalf of two publishing houses,

Tokuma Shoten and Shinchōsha, respectively, as a double bill (McCarthy 1999, 116–7; Suzuki 2013, 39–45).

Joe Hisaishi: A Biographical Sketch

Born as Fujisawa Mamoru on December 6, 1950, in Nagano Prefecture in the mountains of central Japan, Hisaishi studied composition at Kunitachi College of Music, the oldest private music school in Tokyo, founded in 1926. While there, Hisaishi became captivated by the then cutting-edge, avant-garde movement of minimalism after listening to Terry Riley's *A Rainbow in Curved Air* (1968) (Hisaishi 1992, 177). After graduating from Kunitachi, he pursued a career as a composer-performer of minimalist music while taking on odd jobs, teaching piano to children, making orchestral arrangements for concerts, and providing music for the TV anime series, *First Humans Giatrus* (*Hajime ningen gyātoruzu*, 1974–1975).[4] Around this time, he adopted the professional name Joe Hisaishi, a clever play on the name of American producer Quincy Jones.[5] After composing, recording, and producing the album *Mkwaju* (1981), consisting of six minimalist style pieces for percussions and electronic instruments, Hisaishi retired from the world of "modern music" (*gendai ongaku*) and turned a new leaf in his life as a popular music artist. In 1982, he released the album *Information* with his newly formed synth-pop group, Wonder City Orchestra, through the label Japan Record, which was affiliated with Tokuma Japan Communications.

In the summer of 1983, Hisaishi had a fateful meeting with Miyazaki to discuss the "image album" (*imēji arubamu*) for the film, *Nausicaä of the Valley of the Wind* (Takahata 1991, 318–26; Hisaishi 1992, 36–56). An image album is a collection of music based on characters, events, locales, and themes from the film to be sold in advance of the film (Bellano 2010, 5; Koizumi 2010, 62). Anime production companies had begun to pay attention to soundtrack albums as possible sources of revenue following the release of *The Symphonic Suite: Space Battleship Yamato* (*Kōkyōkumikyoku Uchū Senkan Yamato*) in 1977 (Yamasaki 2014, 194).[6] By the time Miyazaki met with Hisaishi, the media mix strategy of creating an album consisting of music based on popular manga series had become a firmly established practice.[7] Takahata, who acted as the music director of *Nausicaä of the Valley of the Wind*, anticipated that such an album for the feature-length animated film could enable him to check the quality and fit of the music by the chosen composer. At the same time, the album could function as an advanced promotional material for future audience members of the film (Suzuki 2011, 74).

Tokuma Japan Communications, the record company owned by Tokuma Shoten, recommended Hisaishi to Takahata and Miyazaki; Tokuma Shoten also published the *Animage* magazine that ran Miyazaki's manga version of *Nausicaä of the Valley of the Wind*. Miyazaki showed Hisaishi the image boards he had created for the *Nausicaä* project and verbally described the characters, objects, events, and situations he had in mind for the film. Hisaishi quickly produced a collection of instrumental music based on Miyazaki's ideas. The album was sold under Tokuma Japan Communications' Animage Records label later that year. When it was time to decide the composer for the soundtrack of the film, both Miyazaki and Takahata pushed for Hisaishi against other composers recommended by Tokuma Shoten's executives. Thanks to Miyazaki and Takahata's insistence, Hisaishi secured the job, providing music for the soundtrack largely based on the music he had composed for the image album.[8]

In his recollections, Takahata (1991, 325) expresses his amazement at how well Hisaishi's music evoked the fantastic world depicted in Miyazaki's film. Considering that Miyazaki had repeatedly listened to Hisaishi's compositions on the image album while he was creating the film, Takahata suspects that the director had fashioned his film in such a way as to work well with Hisaishi's musical ideas. The function of Hisaishi's image album was thus more than promotional: not only did it allow Hisaishi to try out musical ideas during the production phase of the film, but it also provided a rich source of inspiration for Miyazaki's imagination (Bellano 2012). The collaboration between the two artists continued in Miyazaki's next project, *Castle in the Sky*, for which Hisaishi provided both the image album and the music for the film soundtrack. In addition to the image albums, the record company also released newly composed music for the soundtracks of both films as "soundtrack albums" during their initial runs.

The Process of Collaboration

Once he had decided to work on *My Neighbor Totoro*, Miyazaki quickly expressed his desire to have Hisaishi compose the music for the film. Hisaishi, in turn, gladly accepted Miyazaki's request, but he proposed creating a collection of "image songs" instead of the customary image album of instrumental music (Watanabe [1987] 2018, 1). Miyazaki, who felt the need for songs that would appeal to young children, approached Nakagawa whom he had admired since his college days. Recalling their previous collaboration on the theme song for *Castle in the Sky*, "Carrying You" (Kimi o nosete), Hisaishi requested that Miyazaki write additional poems for the album (Hisaishi 1992, 63–64). On April 16, 1987, Miyazaki arranged an interview (*taidan*) with Nakagawa to explain his ideas about the film and formally request her participation in the project. The transcript of the interview was published in the June issue of *Animage* magazine, which represents a shrewd promotional strategy from the magazine editor. Miyazaki was successful in obtaining Nakagawa's interest, initiating a remarkable collaboration among these three creative artists that would last for the next several months. Throughout the process, Suzuki Toshio, who was then the assistant editor of *Animage*, worked as a crucial member of the team, arranging meetings and smoothing out disagreements (Suzuki 2013, 53–55). For the most part, Hisaishi set the poems presented by Nakagawa based on her impression of Miyazaki's narrative. In a few cases, the process was reversed, with Miyazaki adding lyrics to music composed by Hisaishi. In either case, the creation of the image album involved the team working in close partnership.

At the end of the interview published in *Animage*, the unnamed editor of the magazine predicts that "by the fall of this year, one step ahead of the release of the film, it will be possible to hear with our ears the delightful world of *My Neighbor Totoro*" (Miyazaki and Nakagawa 1987, 31). As anticipated, the music inspired by Miyazaki's vision of *My*

Neighbor Totoro became available to the curious public well in advance of the completion of the film. On October 25, Animage Records, another Tokuma Shoten subsidiary, released the 7" vinyl single, "My Neighbor Totoro" (Tonari no Totoro), an instantaneously recognizable, cheerful song based on a poem by Miyazaki and sung by the young idol singer Inoue Azumi, who had become famous for singing the theme song for *Castle in the Sky*. In fact, the B-side of the new single contained a reissue of that very theme song, "Carrying You." The pairing of the new theme song with an already popular one was another clever marketing ploy, which ensured that it would attract the interest of fans of Hisaishi's *Castle in the Sky* and Inoue's singing. However, the release of the single on vinyl and CD in the following year paired "My Neighbor Totoro" with the opening theme song for the new film, "Hey Let's Go" (Sanpo). Tokuma Shoten's strategy to promote the film through music coincided with developments in the Japanese animation and music industries in the 1980s that resulted in a thriving market for animation-related music (Yamasaki 2010, 209).

On November 25, a month after the debut of the image single and almost five months before the release of the film, Animage Records issued the *My Neighbor Totoro: Image Song Collection* (Imēji songu shū) on multiple platforms including LP, cassette, and CD containing the complete set of songs composed by Hisaishi. The album contains eleven pieces in total with lyrics written by Nakagawa, Miyazaki, and W. City Production Team [W. City Seisakubu], and music composed by Hisaishi. Multiple people performed the songs including Inoue, Suginami Children's Chorus, Kitahara Taku, Mori Kumiko, and Hisaishi himself (see the Track List for more information).

The designation of the album as an "image song collection" rather than an "image album" foregrounds the idea that this is a collection of songs. In fact, the original LP release contained a booklet that included the reprint of the dialogue between Miyazaki and Nakagawa, as well as the lyrics and score for all of the songs. That is to say, the image album included a literal "song collection" (*kashū*). However, the score contains only the vocal melody and chord symbols, and it does not always match what is included on the recording. Instrumental passages, introductions, interludes, and codas are cut or abbreviated, and in some cases, even the vocal introductions are eliminated from the sheet music. The sheet music, then, is not necessarily included for the consumers to reproduce the music as heard on the recording, but rather, for them to sing along with it.

Once the image album was completed, Hisaishi, Miyazaki, and Shiba Shigeharu, the sound engineer, began discussing musical cues for the soundtrack of the film (in his 2006 book, Hisaishi calls such meetings "M meetings," or "M uchi"; 84–86).[9] As in his previous two collaborations with Miyazaki, Hisaishi drew on many musical ideas for the soundtrack from his *Image Song Collection*. He rearranged some songs, turning them into instrumental cues, recomposed existing songs into radically different cues, or composed completely new music for the film. At some point during this process, Hisaishi (1992, 69) was hospitalized following a stomach ulcer, which prevented him from producing additional cues on the synthesizer (Hisaishi 1988, 149). Perhaps because of his illness, a second composer, Hirabe Yayoi, was hired to produce additional orchestral arrangements based on Hisaishi's music. According to the liner notes included in the *Soundtrack Collection*, these and other orchestral cues were recorded over a period of four weeks, between February 25 and March 26 in Tokyo. During the mixing stage, in which Miyazaki also participated, Hisaishi introduced additional changes to the cues that he had prepared, in response to Miyazaki's directions. Hisaishi (1988, 149) was in the habit of providing more music than necessary and fully intended some pieces or parts of pieces to be "thinned out."

On May 1, 1988, during the initial run of the film, *My Neighbor Totoro: Soundtrack Collection* was released with twenty items, all composed by Hisaishi. Many pieces included in the album are longer versions of the actual cues included on the soundtrack of the film. These discrepancies suggest that some of the tracks included on the soundtrack album are earlier versions of the cues prepared for the film prior to the mixing stage. Parts of these cues were edited out during the process of mixing. One track, the instrumental version of "The Path of the Wind" (Kaze no tōrimichi, *Image Song Collection*, track 11), was carried over from the image song album (*Soundtrack Collection*, track 13). (Hereafter, tracks are identified with numbers preceded by "I" for tracks from *Image Song Collection* and "S" for tracks from *Soundtrack Collection*, for example, I-11 and S-13 for the items above.) Although there are several cues based on this image song, this particular version of the tune does not appear exactly in this form on the film soundtrack. The soundtrack album includes several songs, not all of which appear on the soundtrack of the actual film. Two of them, both sung by Inoue, "Hey Let's Go: Opening Theme Song" (Sanpo ~ ōpuningu shudaika, S-1) and "My Neighbor Totoro: Ending Theme Song" (Tonari no Totoro ~ Endingu shudaika, S-19), are included in the film soundtrack but in slightly modified versions. The album also contains Inoue's recording of "A Lost Child" (Maigo, S-12), which appears in the film only as instrumental cues. Finally, the album also includes a boisterous arrangement of "Hey Let's Go (with Chorus)" (Sanpo [Gasshō tsuki], S-20) made by Takeichi Masahisa featuring the solo singing of Inoue accompanied by the Suginami Children's Chorus.

* * *

Tokuma Shoten and its subsidiaries have continued to produce and market new musical products related to *My Neighbor Totoro* (see Discography). Two additional arrangements of Hisaishi's music for *My Neighbor Totoro* appeared soon after the release of the film: a so-called "sound book" (saundo bukku) for a small chamber ensemble of acoustic instruments (violin, flute, and guitar) in 1988, and another by Nobuta Kazuo, featuring synthesizers and inspired by traditional music from around the world as part of the Ghibli "high-tech series" (haitekku shirīzu) in 1990. In 2002, a symphonic arrangement of the music from *My Neighbor Totoro* appeared as part of the "orchestra series." Very recently, on November 3, 2018, the Studio Ghibli Records label reissued the image album and the soundtrack album in vinyl with reproductions of the original cover design, liner notes, and even advertisement wrapping (*obi*). The liner notes for the image album include the lyrics and sheet music for the songs included on the album, which are not included in the booklet accompanying the CD version of the album.

The large number of musical products related to *My Neighbor Totoro* points to the important role that music plays in the lasting popularity of the film, as well as the symbiotic relationship between the animation and music industries in Japan. For the fans of the film and music, listening to various composers' arrangements of these familiar tunes provides great pleasure, presenting new and fresh opportunities to fall in love with the music from *My Neighbor Totoro* again and again. However, renewing our attention to the relationship among the three related but distinct multimedia "texts" of *My Neighbor Totoro*—the film, the image album, and the soundtrack album—helps us to better understand the creative process of Miyazaki and Hisaishi that gave the film its distinct sonic and musical signature.

2 Two Songs from the Image Album

In an addendum to the "Project Plan," Miyazaki expresses his wish to include two songs on the soundtrack of the film. He describes the first song as "a lively and simple song suitable for the opening" that encourages children watching the film "to open their mouths as wide as possible and sing at the top of their lungs" (Miyazaki 1996, 402–403). This idea would eventually materialize in the form of the cheerful and energetic image song, "Hey Let's Go." Miyazaki describes the second song as a "touching song" that "children can sing along like a *shōka*" (403). The word *shōka* refers to a genre of songs initially developed for the national education program in Japan by the Ministry of Education (Monbushō), as well as by individual music educators, starting in the Meiji period (1868–1912) (Manabe 2009, 52).[1] Miyazaki's comparison of the song to a *shōka* further reinforces the idea of children singing in unison, since it is still common for children (and adults) to sing *shōka* together in contemporary Japan. The song that came out of this idea is the tuneful but slightly melancholic image song, "My Neighbor Totoro." These two songs, both designed to move children to sing, stood at the center of Miyazaki's sonic conception for the film.

As they were among the first music from the film that the public heard, these two songs colored the ways in which early Japanese audiences engaged with the film. Furthermore, they convey important messages that Miyazaki hoped to address in the film at the earliest stages of planning. In this chapter, I listen closely to these two image songs as a way of highlighting the themes that Miyazaki brings to his film. In the process, the director's hidden appeal to the emotional power of nostalgia invites us to listen to the song and watch the film repeatedly, over and over, without ever becoming bored.

"My Neighbor Totoro" (I-1): A Song Rich in Nuance

According to his 1992 autobiography, *I Am: Toward the Distant Path of Music* (*I Am: Haruka naru ongaku no michi e*), the melody for "My Neighbor Totoro" (I-1) came to Hisaishi by accident while he was muttering the name "Totoro" repeatedly in the bathtub "as if reciting a magical incantation" (Hisaishi 1992, 64). Suddenly, a musical phrase came to him which would eventually turn into the familiar refrain "Totoro Totoro Totoro Totoro." In his recently published recollection of his work for *My Neighbor Totoro*, production staff member Kihara Hirokatsu (2018, 183) explains that the song actually started with Hisaishi's "demo music" (recordings containing basic musical ideas to be elaborated and refined later) to which Miyazaki added the lyrics.[2] Because we know that Miyazaki, Nakagawa, and Hisaishi met multiple times over the course of several months as they planned their album, it is likely that

Hisaishi also adjusted his music to Miyazaki's lyrics as they came into being. Indeed, Hisaishi (1992, 65) writes that because he found Miyazaki's words to be "pure and direct," he decided to create a song that is "rich in nuance" but resembles a "*dōyō*," a kind of piece that "children can sing in a loud voice using all of their might."

While Hisaishi's sentiment resonates with Miyazaki's call for a *shōka*-like children's song, the term that Hisaishi uses to describe it—*dōyō*—is different. In fact, *dōyō* refers to a genre of children's songs developed in the Taishō period (1912–1926) by Japanese poets and composers, partly in search of artistic expression, and partly to respond to the emotional needs and desires of actual children (Manabe 2009, 173). Considering Miyazaki's repeated call to create a work that appeals to the lives and experiences of children, Hisaishi's allusion to *dōyō* in this passage captures the spirit of Miyazaki's intent better than *shōka*. What Hisaishi created in the end was a memorable and beloved image song "My Neighbor Totoro," which not only answered Miyazaki's call for a song suitable for children's singing but also musically captured one of the film's central themes: the boundary between reality and magic that children alone are able to cross (Cavallaro 2015, 29; Napier 2018, 110).

Even though writing music for children was a brand new experience for the composer, Hisaishi's "My Neighbor Totoro" contains important hallmarks of his personal style that he had been cultivating for over two decades. Hisaishi himself (1992, 136) distinguishes two features of his music: "Hisaishi melody" and "minimal and ethnic." Noting that "Hisaishi melody" is commonly used to refer to the composer's melodies, musicologist Alexandra Roedder (2013, 40–43) characterizes this melody, based on her interview with the composer, as having evenly shaped phrases in a narrow range, often laid out in a predictable AABA form. I would add that the composer's penchant for descending third sequence, chromatic harmonies, and extended chords are an important component of the Hisaishi melody.[3] Hisaishi (1992, 136) himself describes "minimal and ethnic" as an approach that is more concerned with "sound" rather than "pretty melody." The term "minimal and ethnic" also reflects Hisaishi's interest in American minimalist composers, especially Terry Riley, Steve Reich, and Philip Glass, all of whom, at one point or another, sought inspiration from the musical traditions from Asia and Africa (Schwartz 1996, 9).

Although Hisaishi himself conceives of these two "faces" in an oppositional relationship, elements from both appear in the song "My Neighbor Totoro." The image song opens with a brief but lively instrumental introduction in the "minimal and ethnic" style; this introduction leads to a simple refrain consisting of a fourfold repetition of the name Totoro, just as it had come to Hisaishi's mind in the bathtub. This two-measure-long introduction features three types of pitched and unpitched percussion instruments, playing brief repetitive melodic and rhythmic patterns that overlap with each other to create a rich tapestry of sound. In this and other pieces, Hisaishi freely combines sounds of acoustic instruments and sounds created by synthesizers and samplers, making the identification of instruments somewhat challenging. Nevertheless, the timbre of the pitched instrument resembles that of the marimba, and one of the two unpitched instruments sounds like the dry, pleasant sound of a wood block. To this, Hisaishi adds the flexible sounds of what sounds like a tabla, an instrument Hisaishi (1988, 149) recalls sampling himself.

Above this minimalist instrumental texture, Inoue and an uncredited chorus of male voices sing the refrain, the fourfold incantation of the name "Totoro" (Example 1). The refrain consists of a series of falling gestures, each set to the name "Totoro." Hisaishi arranges these gestures so that the third and fourth follow the first and second a step lower. What complicates this plain melodic scheme, however, is the rhythm. The first gesture starts on the downbeat of the measure in 4/4 time, grounding the melody on a secure rhythmic footing. But Hisaishi quickly introduces syncopation, starting the second statement of "Totoro" on an offbeat (the second half of the third beat), disrupting the metric regularity of the first statement. The composer elongates the rhythmic value of the second syllable of "To-<u>to</u>-ro" from eight note to a quarter note, so that the note is sung across the bar line, creating a pleasantly syncopated rhythm. This rhythmic pattern is repeated again for the last two statements of "Totoro," creating a distinct impression of rhythmic playfulness, as if we are tiptoeing on an uneven surface, constantly trying to adjust our balance. The syncopated rhythm that Hisaishi introduces here is another hallmark of his "minimal and ethnic" style, but

Example 1 *"My Neighbor Totoro" (I-1, 0:04), "Totoro Refrain".*

it is uncharacteristic of traditional *shōka*, which tend to feature melodies with regular and predictable rhythmic profiles.[4]

Hisaishi's unexpected harmonization of the refrain, on the other hand, points to the style of the Hisaishi melody. The refrain begins on the tonic chord (F) in the key of F major and moves to the dominant chord (C7) in the second measure. The third measure reiterates the same chord, and at this point, Hisaishi could have easily harmonized the melody with a shift back to F in the fourth measure. Instead, he throws in a chromatic harmony in the second half of the third measure (C♯-diminished) that leads the harmony to D minor instead of F in the fourth measure. The harmonic sleight of hand results in a deceptive motion that concludes the refrain on an unexpected minor chord. The introduction of the chromatic harmony in the third measure also modifies the established harmonic rhythm, or the rate at which the chords change. The gesture suggests a change in the mood of the refrain to something more wistful and bittersweet, setting up the general emotional tone of the film as a whole. A lively instrumental transition section, however, reinstates the cheerful mood, driving away any lingering melancholic feelings, at least for a brief moment.

Hisaishi continues to balance two compositional imperatives of a tune that is both easy to sing and rich in nuance in the verse and chorus of the song. Hisaishi confines the range of the melody to a relatively narrow range of a minor tenth. As in many *shōka*, the melody is almost entirely syllabic (one note per syllable) and is devoid of difficult runs. It unfolds largely in stepwise motion with small leaps, except for occasional large leaps designed to coincide with important words and phrases.

For instance, in the climactic moment of the first chorus, the melody jumps by an octave to the word "child" (*kodomo*) (I-1, 1:18). Rhythmically, however, Hisaishi continues to work with his characteristic syncopated rhythmic flair, already heard in the introduction, throughout the melody of the verse and chorus as well as the accompaniment. Hisaishi's jerky but pleasantly lively rhythmic pattern creates a peculiar sense of being simultaneously behind and ahead of time.

The melody of the image song remains almost entirely diatonic. Harmonically, however, Hisaishi adds chromatic chords and extended chords in line with the style of the Hisaishi melody. Hisaishi has already introduced a chromatic chord in the refrain. In the verse section, Hisaishi places additional chromatic chords starting in the second line, where he presents two chords side by side, B♭ and B♭m6 (0:27–0:30). The second chord sounds unexpected because it belongs not to the prevailing tonality of the piece but, instead, to the key of F *minor*. This is an example of modal mixture, the practice of borrowing notes and chords that belong to a major or minor key with the same tonic, which Hisaishi uses frequently throughout this album. The phrase concludes with, Gm7/C, an extended chord (V11) that points to the harmonic vocabulary of contemporary jazz and pop musicians rather than historic *shōka* or *dōyō*. In the subsequent lines of the verse, Hisaishi introduces additional chromatic harmonies that constantly suggest tonal shifts to G minor (D7 at 0:41) and F minor (B♭m6 at 0:44). By the final line of the verse (0:49), however, the harmonic rhythm slows down, and tonality returns to F major, closing on the extended dominant harmony Gm7/C (0:53) that prepares for the chorus.

Hisaishi continues to pepper his music with unexpected chromatic harmonies in the chorus section of "My Neighbor Totoro." The chorus opens with the familiar refrain, the four-part repetition of the name "Totoro" preceded by the phrase "next door" (*tonari no*). The second line of the chorus opens with a quarter rest followed by a D♭ in the vocal part over B♭m (1:04), another instance of modal mixture. Although Hisaishi deploys chromatic harmonies throughout the song, this is the only instance of a chromatic pitch in the sung melody. From a practical standpoint, singing this note can be challenging since it does not belong to the key of F major. In the following line, Hisaishi repeats the Totoro refrain. Based on the established pattern, the audience is encouraged to anticipate the fourth line to start on a quarter rest followed by the chromatic pitch D♭. However, the composer undercuts this expectation by starting the fourth line on the downbeat on D above a B♭ that negates the earlier chromatic alteration presented (1:19). As if to revel in this happy resolution, Inoue's voice leaps up by an octave, pushing the melody of the song to its highest point so far. The final line of the chorus concludes with a clear tonal closure in F major followed by a leisurely interlude that prepares for the entrance of the second verse (1:27).

The concluding section of the image song starts with a sudden tonal shift from F major up to G♭ major (2:57). This kind of upward tonal shift by a half step is a common gesture in popular music, heightening the excitement. This section repeats the first chorus of the song, followed immediately by the coda (3:30) consisting of the "Totoro" refrain, stated not once but six times as the music fades out. The frequency with which the name Totoro is repeated (twenty-four times in the coda alone) perhaps reflects Hisaishi's response to Miyazaki's wish for a song that children could easily sing. As discussed earlier, the verse and chorus sections contain complicated rhythmic figures and chromatic notes. By comparison, the coda consists of the single word "Totoro," which children of all ages could conceivably sing along without much trouble. The frequent repetition of the name Totoro evokes children's songs that revel in the repeated utterances of nonsense syllables, adding to the sense of innocence. Yet, the repetition also ends up emphasizing the chromatic harmony that leads to a deceptive motion in this otherwise simple musical passage. Perhaps because the Totoro refrain does not end on the tonic harmony, the metaphorical "home" of the song, we feel compelled to repeat it endlessly in the hope of reaching the longed-for tonal resolution. In other words, the structure of the song captures the emotional trajectory of nostalgia understood as homesickness.

In addition to providing the musical nuance that balances out the simplicity of Miyazaki's poem, the harmonic uncertainties that Hisaishi introduces in the song highlight an important aspect of Miyazaki's vision for *My Neighbor Totoro*. In her recent book on Miyazaki, Susan Napier (2018, 110) argues that the film "emblemizes a type of fantastic structure" that leaves the viewers with the feeling of "the betwixt and between," unable to decide whether events unfolding in front of them have "supernatural or realistic explanations." While Miyazaki and his creative team spent a vast amount of time and resources to assiduously recreate the visual and sonic environments of the late 1950s, the film also dwells on creating an imaginary world in which supernatural creatures exist side by side with humans. In particular, Miyazaki's lyrics for "My Neighbor Totoro" teach us to read various signs of nature as secret keys necessary to slip into the magical world of Totoro. The lines in the first verse, for instance, explain that an acorn sprouting in the middle of a road actually turns out to be "a secret code" and "a passport to the forest," which signals the beginning of a "wonderful adventure." Miyazaki introduces the figure of Totoro in the chorus and muses that such a mysterious encounter "visits you" only in one's childhood. The first five lines of the second verse allude to an iconic scene from the film: Satsuki's curious encounter with a "soaking-wet monster" at the bus stop that initiates, in the film, Satsuki's introduction to the magical world of Totoro. Miyazaki once again addresses the listeners in the second chorus, predicting that "a lovely happiness" will come your way if you were to meet Totoro. Miyazaki includes the second person pronoun "you" (*anata*) in both of these passages, as if to suggest that we, too, might be lucky enough to bump into Totoro someday. Yet, Miyazaki also reminds us that such encounters can only happen to children, whose innocence and openness to the world enable them to cross the boundary between reality and fantasy. What Hisaishi reinforces in "My Neighbor Totoro" through its harmonic instability, however, is not the distance between reality and fantasy but, rather, the permeability of the boundary that separates the two. Like Satsuki and Mei who inhabit two worlds at the same time, Hisaishi's subtly complex harmonies for Miyazaki's lyrics slips in and out of different major and minor keys, keeping us guessing where we belong.

"Hey Let's Go" (I-3)

While Hisaishi has an amusing story to tell about the birth of "My Neighbor Totoro," he found adding music to Nakagawa's poems, including "Hey Let's Go," to be almost impossible. In fact, he describes Nakagawa's lyrics as "the kind that makes composers cry" (*sakkyokuka nakase no mono*) because of their simplicity and "straight-forwardness" that lacked the kinds of "sentimental words" typically seen in song lyrics (Hisaishi 1992, 64). Suzuki (2013, 54) also recalls having to cajole Hisaishi, who had initially rejected the lyrics prepared by Nakagawa, into following through with the project. The second volume of the *Archives of Studio Ghibli* (1996, 83) includes an early draft of Nakagawa's lyrics for "Hey Let's Go" with the alternate title, "Strolling Song" (*sanpo no uta*). The volume also includes Hisaishi's musical sketch, consisting of a melody, chord names, and some lyrics. Hisaishi places an open circle under each note head, creating a row of circles. He also inserts texts from Nakagawa's lyrics above and below the row of circles. The document gives us a glimpse into the process of how Hisaishi struggled to reconcile his musical idea with Nakagawa's words. Once the song was completed, it was recorded by Inoue and included on the image album as its third track. As anticipated in the "Project Plans," the song was repurposed as the film's cheerful opening theme song. It has since become one of Hisaishi's most famous and recognizable songs.

While "My Neighbor Totoro" contains arresting poetic as well as musical elements that make it a song "rich in nuance," "Hey Let's Go" (I-3) projects a bright, carefree mood that seems to chase away any negative thoughts. In fact, practically almost every aspect of the image song "Hey Let's Go" can be understood to embody Miyazaki's goal of providing a song that encourages the young children watching the film to sing along in loud, energetic voices. Take Nakagawa's poem, for instance. Written in a simple, unadorned manner devoid of clichés and hackneyed poetic tropes, Nakagawa's lyrics celebrate the pleasure of taking a stroll (*sanpo*), while listing the various obstacles (an incline, a tunnel, a log bridge, etc.) and critters (a bee, a lizard, a snake, etc.) a child might encounter and find exciting. Nakagawa avoids using any abstract concepts, fanciful metaphors, or complicated sentence structures. She also presents the poem using entirely *hiragana* and *katakana* syllabaries, avoiding even the most rudimentary Chinese characters that a typical first grader in Japan would know.[5] In other words, Nakagawa designed her poem to be comprehensible to very young Japanese children.

Mirroring the plainness of Nakagawa's poem, Hisaishi also embraces the idea of simplicity and ease of performance in "Hey Let's Go." The song is in a simple strophic form. It starts in the key of C major and moves up to Db major in the third verse (I-3, 1:48) but remains in 4/4 meter. Hisaishi does not indicate a tempo, but Inoue and the Suginami Children's Chorus's recording on the image album is in a moderately fast tempo suggestive of the brisk walking pace of a child. Hisaishi's vocal melody has a relatively narrow range (a major ninth) and a regular and predictable four-bar phrase structure. In a *shōka* like fashion, the melody also contains very little rhythmic variety, mostly consisting of quarter notes and a swinging dotted eighth plus sixteenth-note pattern. For example, the opening measure of the vocal melody (0:20) contains three notes, E, G, and C, all sung as a series of steady quarter notes that launches the voice upward, outlining a tonic triad (C chord). This simple musical gesture, sung to the word "arukō," a straightforward invitation to take a walk, neatly captures the song's enthusiasm for the activity (Example 2). The same text is repeated in the second measure (0:23) but with a contrasting melodic gesture that starts on G, moves up by a step to A, and returns back to G, sung to the same rhythm. This opening musical gesture not only matches the simplicity of Nakagawa's poem but also seems to invite the young children to sing along "at the top of their lungs," as Miyazaki had fantasized. The text and music of this opening gesture is repeated at the beginning of each verse, making the song even more approachable and memorable.

Nevertheless, below this surface of simplicity lie a few notable elements of the Hisaishi melody. For instance, after presenting the two simple settings of the invocation to walk, Hisaishi increases the speed of text delivery, cramming twice as many syllables in the following measure. A quickening of the harmonic rhythm accompanies this melodic compression. These melodic, harmonic, and rhythmic features provide variety to the first phrase of the song and add forward momentum to the first strain. So far, the melody and harmonies of the song have remained diatonic. However, at the beginning of

Example 2 *"Hey Let's Go" (I-3, 0:20), the opening measures of the sung melody.*

the second strain, in m. 9 on the lead sheet (0:36), Hisaishi introduces an A♭ in the melody, a chromatic note that does not belong to the home key of C major. The chord that supports this wayward pitch is F minor, which comes back two measures later. These instances of modal mixture are fleeting but give an unexpected depth of feeling to this song. Hisaishi also includes some syncopated rhythm toward the end of the verse (mm. 13–14 and mm. 17–18) (0:46 and 0:53) that adds a snappy zest to the song.

As in "My Neighbor Totoro," Inoue sings the third verse up by a half step, from C major to D♭ major, that ramps up the tension and excitement of the piece. The song reaches an optimistic conclusion as the melody climbs steadily in stepwise motion from A♭ to D♭ (2:34), the tonic pitch of the key. As Inoue holds the final note of the song for two full measures, the accompaniment part presents a whole-tone scale with a chromatic passing note at the end (D♭-C♭-A-G-F-E♭-D-D♭).[6] The gesture, although slightly menacing, adds humor to the song before the song comes to an end with an emphatic cadence. The clear ending of the song is in sharp contrast to the ambiguous ending of "My Neighbor Totoro."

Although Miyazaki referred to the song for the opening as neither *shōka* nor *dōyō* in the "Project Plan," his collaborators and commentators often refer to the song in this manner. Kihara (2018, 78) recalls how the director enthusiastically expressed a need for a "*dōyō*-like song that is easy to get used to" for the opening of the film. Notwithstanding Hisaishi's occasional rhythmic and harmonic twists, "Hey Let's Go" contains many stylistic elements of children's songs, including its simple text by Nakagawa. In fact, one review of the image album that appeared in *Animage* discusses the *dōyō*-like feel of the lyrics in the album as a whole. However, the same review also points out Hisaishi's deliberate avoidance of "*dōyō*-esque scales [*dōyō-teki onkai*]," that keeps the music fresh and appealing rather than "nostalgic" (Suishō and Yamamoto 1987, 198). Ironically, however, the popularity of the film and Hisaishi's music grew so much in the years following the release of the film that "Hey Let's Go" has been included in textbooks (Hisaishi 1992, 66) and sung at pre-schools and kindergartens all over Japan ("Sutajio Jiburi monogatari" 2013, 35). In other words, a song that was partly created in imitation of the style of a *shōka* and *dōyō* has now become an actual school song, sung by tens of thousands of Japanese children.

In keeping with Miyazaki's plan, the image song "Hey Let's Go" appears on the soundtrack of the film as the opening theme song, but with significant alterations that reveal a lot about the collaborative process of the director and composer and their attitude toward the role of music in the film. One major alteration to the image song version of "Hey Let's Go" was the elimination of the second verse. Another obvious change was the elimination of the children's chorus and the addition of bagpipes to the introduction of the song. In the image album version of the song, the instrumental introduction only has the sounds of percussion instruments. A bass drum and cymbals beat a steady march rhythm (Long-Long-Short-Short-Long), followed by a brass band playing an ascending scalar passage. Adding bagpipes to the mix was Hisaishi's original idea, which may seem unexpected for a film set in the remote Japanese countryside. The sound of the bagpipes typically brings to mind European folk music, especially from Scotland

and Ireland. However, when Miyazaki heard the new version with the bagpipes, he liked it so much that he wanted Hisaishi to put that sound in "all of it" (Hisaishi 1988, 148). As a result, the bagpipes return throughout the rest of the song in the instrumental interlude between verses, the final verse, and the conclusion of the song.

According to Hisaishi, introducing a foreign musical element to the score of *My Neighbor Totoro* was a natural thing for him. Looking back at his score for *Castle in the Sky*, which was also based on his impression of folk music from the British Isles, Hisaishi (1992, 57) observes: "For modern Japanese, I think English and Irish folksongs are like their foundational musical experience." He justifies this bold statement by pointing out that Japanese school children are introduced to *shōka* that relied on folk songs from this part of the world, taking the Japanese setting of the Scottish folk tune "Auld Lang Syne" as an example. The song continues to be popular in Japan today as "Hotaru no Hikari": it is often sung at graduation ceremonies and heard on loudspeakers in Japanese shopping areas (*shōtengai*) and individual stores at the end of the business day. Although many *shōka* were created by Japanese composers, early published collections of *shōka* included many adaptations of existing melodies from Europe and the United States fitted with newly composed Japanese texts with didactic messages (Manabe 2009, 238). In a more recent collection of essays, Hisaishi (2007, 118) asks the rhetorical question, "Why do I work on Western music (*seiyō ongaku*) even though I am Japanese?" These provocative comments by the composer point to the complexity of the formation of national musical identity in modern Japan.

As in their earlier collaboration, Miyazaki got into the habit of listening and singing along to Hisaishi's image songs as he worked on *My Neighbor Totoro,* including "Hey Let's Go." According to Kihara, however, Miyazaki was fond of replacing the word "[I am] feeling fine" (*genki*) with "badger" (*tanuki*) so that he would sing out the phrase "I am a badger" in jest (Kihara 2018, 183). As Takahata had noted, Kihara recognized that the activity helped Miyazaki to concentrate and produce concrete results.

One example of this is the opening sequence of the film, for which Miyazaki did not provide a story board (Kihara 2018, 79) but instead followed the form of "Hey Let's Go" closely. The instrumental introduction accompanies the opening animation of the march of Small Totoro, followed by the transformation of the seeds, first into nine Small Totoro, and then into a threefold presentation of the name Totoro rendered in *katakana* against a blue background. The first verse of the song, sung in Inoue's inviting, cheerful voice, starts when the main title of the film appears, in white lettering against a tangerine background, with animated decorative borders made up of animals and random objects in the yard. After Inoue's friendly invitation to walk, Mei walks from the right side of the screen to the left in between the borders, followed by various critters (a worm, a grasshopper, and Small Totoro). Although they are not completely identical, the images reinforce Nakagawa's text by alluding to the animals and objects originally included in the song in the opening sequence. The animation of Small Totoro against the blue background returns during the interlude, then transitions to Mei's march for the second and final verse of the song, now sung a half step higher.

While the large-scale structure of the opening sequence matches that of the form of the song, on a more minute level, one might object that the pace of Mei's marching and Small Totoro's motions do not align with the metrical structure of the music, at least in a visibly obvious manner. Later in the book, I will return to the significance of this type of asynchrony between the image and the music in this film that goes against the practice developed in Hollywood. As in the version in the image album, the opening theme song concludes with the quasi whole-tone descending scale, followed by the brass chords and a newly added bagpipe flourish as the screen blacks out. This falling sonic gesture seems to call out to the viewers that something extraordinary is about to happen, anticipating the fall that Mei will make into Totoro's lair at the end of her exploration of her backyard.

* * *

The two image songs, "My Neighbor Totoro" and "Hey Let's Go," embody Miyazaki's wish to create two songs that truly entertain his intended audience and move them to participate in the act of music-making. Furthermore, conceived at an early stage in the planning for the film, the songs capture many of its central themes and its director's concerns. "My Neighbor Totoro," both poetically and musically, explores the permeable boundary between reality and the supernatural realm. The song encourages young children to explore nature with open eyes, ears, and minds. It also reminds grownups of a time when the world seemed simultaneously real and magical, a time when they too may have encountered Totoro. The song calls for a specific kind of nostalgia—a nostalgia for an open attitude to the world that we once had, which could accommodate two seemingly opposing understandings of the world. On the other hand, the emphasis on poetic and musical simplicity in "Hey Let's Go" reflects the collaborative team's deliberate attempt at fashioning a children's song, a modern-day *shōka* and *dōyō*, designed to respond to the emotional and physical needs of young children. The song engages with the idea of nostalgia, partly through its stylistic similarities with this historic repertory of children's music associated with formal school education. It has, in fact, turned into a *shōka* of sorts, thus becoming a source of nostalgia for those who grew up listening to and singing this music as they moved their bodies. Ultimately, both songs resonate with Miyazaki's idealized vision of childhood, centered on physical activity, independence, and interaction with nature.

3 Totoro in Music and Sound

In his 1992 autobiography *I Am,* Hisaishi praises Henry Mancini's score for *Breakfast at Tiffany's* (1961), especially the way that the composer arranged his song "Moon River" to "exactly match the screen" throughout the film. In fact, Hisaishi (1992, 142–43) considers "Moon River" to be an example of a highly successful "main theme" in a film soundtrack, because it binds disparate segments of the film together into an organically unified whole through its appearance in multiple guises, both instrumental and vocal, accommodating the particular dramatic requirements of any given scene.[1] Hisaishi himself uses various arrangements, both instrumental and vocal, of the theme song, "Carrying You" in the soundtrack for *Castle in the Sky.* For *My Neighbor Totoro*, however, Hisaishi prepared not one but *two* compositions that fit the composer's description of the "main theme": "My Neighbor Totoro" and "Totoro's Theme." Tuneful and lively, "My Neighbor Totoro" described in some detail in Chapter 2, conveys a range of positive sentiments that encapsulate the girls' feelings toward the creatures in a familiar musical style. "Totoro's Theme," on the other hand, is a curious musical composition devoid of melody in any conventional sense. Instead, the music consists of layers of repetitive sonic cells mixing the sounds of acoustic and synthesized instruments, evocative of Hisaishi's earlier, minimalist compositions.

On the surface, having two main themes in contrasting styles may seem to negate the sense of organic unity that Hisaishi prizes in his film scores. However, I argue that Hisaishi's juxtaposition of these pieces reinforces the duality that Miyazaki saw in the figure of Totoro as a creature that is simultaneously real and fantastical. The remainder of this chapter analyzes the music and sound from four crucial moments in the film that dramatize the various interactions between Satsuki and Mei and the trio of Totoro: Mei's initial encounter (*deai*) with the three Totoro during her exploration of the yard, Satsuki's encounter with Large Totoro at a bus stop, the magical flight through the moonlit night, and Mei's rescue at the climax of the film. These scenes all treat the perception of the world as both real and fantastical—an important theme, as discussed in Chapter 2. Because such an understanding of the world is associated with childhood, Mei's and Satsuki's interaction with Totoro, supported by Hisaishi's music, appeals to the viewers' sense of nostalgia for their own childhood. As it has done for centuries, music endows this longing with visceral urgency.

Mei Meets Totoro

One morning, after her big sister completes her morning chores and leaves home for school, Mei decides to embark on a solo adventure in the backyard while her father works in his study. Mei's attention shifts rapidly from gathering wildflowers for her father to trying to catch tadpoles and collecting shiny acorns among the tall weeds. To enhance the mood of this delightful and exciting sequence, Hisaishi composed one of his longest cues for the film. Included on the soundtrack album with the title, "The Little Monster" (Chiisana obake, S-9), this cue relies on the familiar audiovisual technique called "mickey-mousing" (Roedder 2013, 130). The term "mickey-mousing" refers to "the exact synchronization of music and actions" (Goldmark 2005, 6) or the scoring practice of "following the visual action in synchrony with musical trajectories (rising, falling, zigzagging) and instrumental punctuation of action (blows, falls, doors closing)" (Chion 1994, 121–22), exemplified by the Disney cartoons featuring its namesake. The practice necessitated the process in which the composer creates the music alongside film production or after it, with the aim of matching the music to the actions depicted on the screen. Despite its ubiquity in cartoons and animations, Hisaishi himself finds the technique "distasteful" (Roedder 2013, 128). In fact, his use of the technique in this particular cue is a departure from his customary compositional strategy for Studio Ghibli films, which relies on preexisting compositions from the image albums (Bellano 2012, 11). In an interview, Hisaishi (1988, 149) recalls that recording this cue took the longest because of the challenges of managing over fifty instances where the music, supplied by an orchestra, and the image had to be coordinated with each other. As a result of this process, the mickey-mousing in this passage, together with the judicious insertion of sound effects, creates a humorous chase sequence that stands out from the rest of the film.

Hisaishi's cue starts with a shot of Mei, who peers into a puddle at the bottom of a dried-up pond and finds tadpoles [0:27:51 on the film]. From then on, Hisaishi supplies a musical gesture to match every movement that Mei makes as she scampers around the backyard in delight. When Mei spots a pair of pointy white ears sticking out of the tall grass in front of her, the music suddenly turns to the refrain from "My Neighbor Totoro" [0:28:56] (Roedder 2013, 130). The words attached to this instrumental phrase in the image song are "Totoro Totoro Totoro Totoro." To an audience familiar with the song, the phrase signals the identity of the owner of these pointy ears. This connection is confirmed when the camera shows the semitranslucent Small Totoro waddling leisurely along the path. In this instance, the phrase functions as a leitmotif—a musical idea or a theme, often brief but memorable, which represents a character, a place, an event, or a more abstract idea, repeated, arranged, and developed to provide additional information to the attentive viewer.

Throughout the remainder of the cue, Hisaishi develops the refrain in different guises to match the events unfolding on the screen. For instance, once Mei starts to follow the mysterious creature, the refrain turns into a jolly march [0:29:12]. However, when Small Totoro becomes aware of Mei and makes itself invisible, the march ends abruptly [0:29:22]. The cue turns into nondescript music, consisting of a rhythmic pulsing on the marimba over a sustained string chord conveying Mei's bewilderment. But when Mei focuses her mind and somehow manages to see the invisible creature, the theme returns with a renewed vigor [0:29:32]. The French horns, an instrument traditionally associated with the hunt in Western tradition, blares out the first four notes of the melody as Mei chases the creature. As the chase continues, Hisaishi repeats this four-note fragment over a frantic accompaniment suggestive of the urgency of the situation.

Eventually, Small Totoro runs into the crawlspace of the house and escapes from Mei's reach. After trying and failing to squeeze herself through the wooden grates, Mei decides to go around the house to another opening, where she waits for Totoro to come out. The music changes again to match the mood of this scene. The tempo becomes slower, and the dynamics are lowered. Most notably, Hisaishi transforms the Totoro refrain to fit the whole-tone scale, suggesting the suspension of time and the supernatural [0:30:15] (Example 3). Two additional statements of the Totoro refrain appear in the remainder of the cue. The first is when Mei discovers Small Totoro and Medium Totoro sneaking behind her and starts to chase after them [0:30:43]. Hisaishi assigns the melody to the trumpet over a brisk march-like accompaniment. The last appearance comes when Mei chases the creatures into the tunnel formed by the shrubbery, which leads to the camphor tree [0:31:16]. The accelerated pace of the melody is suggestive of the mounting excitement as the hunt nears its end. Hisaishi abandons mickey-mousing, however, when the camera cuts to show the two Totoro and Mei scurrying across the surface of the knotty roots of the camphor tree [0:31:25] (Roedder 2013, 131). The cue switches to an instrumental rendition of the image song, "The Path of the Wind," discussed in the next chapter. The relaxed tempo and the wistful melody of the cue fail to convey the tense final moment of Mei's pursuit of the Totoro. The music lasts only for about sixteen seconds and

Example 3 *Whole-tone transformation of "Totoro Refrain" [0:30:15].*

melts away without creating a clear sense of closure, bringing the chase to an abrupt and unsatisfactory end.

Mei loses sight of the two Totoro at the bottom of the camphor tree but spots a shiny acorn hidden within the deep creases of its roots. Ever the intrepid adventurer, Mei reaches for an acorn lodged deep inside an opening on the surface of the tree and falls into a tunnel leading to a large hollow inside the tree. The floor and walls of the space are covered in green mosses, ferns, wildflowers, and other sorts of vegetation. From the opening at the top of the hollow, the thick branches of the camphor tree are visible. The camera cuts and shows a gigantic, brownish-gray, fluffy mass perched in an alcove. This is Large Totoro, asleep inside its lair.

To set the mood of suspense and mystery at this moment, Hisaishi introduces strangely sparse music. Hisaishi calls this "Totoro's Theme" in the featurette "Scoring Miyazaki," included in the 2010 Disney DVD release of *My Neighbor Totoro*. Considering its dramatic significance, Hisaishi did not think adding sound effects alone to the scene would be sufficient. The solution was to include some music, but he wanted to compose something "unobtrusive like air." A fully realized version of "Totoro's Theme" can be heard on the soundtrack album in the first half of the track simply titled "Totoro" (S-10). It is Hisaishi's take on a minimalist composition, consisting of repeated cycles of heterogeneous musical materials including a slightly reverberating synthesized pitch, a group of pulsing open fourths, a two-note marimba fragment, a single *staccato* synthesized vocal note, and overlapping lines of synthesized vocal utterances. Hisaishi alters and develops these musical materials throughout the composition, creating a piece that seems to evolve freely and organically.

For Mei's encounter with Totoro in the film, Hisaishi strips down the composition to strands of sustained synthesized vocal tones that come in and out independently of each other, uttering the syllable "ah" to create a series of shifting, consonant harmonies [0:32:05].[2] The cue points to the lasting impact that Brian Eno's *Ambient 1: Music for Airports* (1978) had on the composer since he encountered it during his minimalist years (Hisaishi 1992, 195). The cue in *Totoro* is extremely brief, lasting for just under thirty seconds. It is quite soft, easily overpowered by the rustling of the grasses that Mei makes. Despite these constraints, this strange soundscape conveys a sense of mystery and wonderment that sets the stage for Mei's first encounter with Large Totoro. This simple, brief, and almost inaudible cue of synthesized sounds creates a maximal contrast with the music in the previous chase scene, which was elaborate, lengthy, loud, and recorded by a live symphonic orchestra.

The next series of events, in which Mei attempts to have a conversation with the bemused Totoro, takes place without any music. Instead, the sound of the wind pervades the scene every time Totoro makes its incomprehensible utterances. Shiba (1988, 147), the film's sound director, recalls in an interview that he engineered the "voice" of Large Totoro by first lowering the recorded vocal pitch of the voice actor and mixing it with the sound of the wind. After having named the creature "Totoro," Mei begins to relax and falls asleep lying on top of Totoro. A new arrangement of the verse section of "My Neighbor Totoro," also included at the end of the track "Totoro" on the soundtrack album (S-10, from 1:57), enters at this point [0:35:18]. This orchestral-strings arrangement (by Hirabe) presents a rich contrapuntal texture that weaves the melody together with a new countermelody and an active bass line. The music envelopes the moment of peace and comfort that Mei now finds with Totoro. It continues across the next few cuts, which show idyllic scenes of an afternoon on an early summer's day, and winds down when Satsuki's return home announces our own return to reality. The cue is included on the soundtrack album as the second half of the track "Totoro."

That evening, Satsuki writes a letter to her mother summarizing Mei's adventures and wishing that she can also one day meet the Totoro. A sound that resembles the hooting of an owl accompanies Satsuki's musings, but it sounds suspiciously like the Totoro refrain [0:41:19]. The scene cuts to the trio of Totoro perched on a branch of a tree blowing on the ocarinas, just as described in the song "My Neighbor Totoro." Because Satsuki's voice is heard as a voice-over, and the camera focuses on Satsuki daydreaming as she writes the letter, it is not clear if this vision and the music is an imagined one in Satsuki's mind, or the Totoro are actually playing the ocarina.

Satsuki Meets Totoro

Luckily for Satsuki, her dream of meeting Totoro comes true quickly. The encounter takes place on one rainy evening at a desolate bus stop at the edge of the forest as the sisters wait for the return of their father. For a long time, the forest remains silent except for the sound of the falling rain. Suddenly, Satsuki notices strange footsteps approaching her. Her vision is limited because she has to balance the umbrella on her shoulder while she carries Mei on her back. She sees a pair of stubby gray-brown legs with frightfully long claws coming toward her. The creature stops and turns away from her. She tilts her head and sees the giant Totoro wearing a piece of yam leaf on its head. Satsuki asks if the creature is Totoro; it utters an indecipherable groan, which she takes to be a positive answer. She then offers the umbrella that she had brought for her father demonstrating how to use it. Totoro holds the umbrella above its head. The cue that Hisaishi inserts at this point is another version of Totoro's theme, but one that is much more elaborate than the cue first heard during Mei's encounter with Large Totoro in the lair [0:50:45]. As in Mei's scene with Totoro, Hisaishi's music here is subtle, blending smoothly with the ambient soundscape consisting of the sounds of raindrops, Totoro's footsteps, Totoro's groans, and Satsuki's gasps.

In an interview included in the *Ghibli Roman Album*, Miyazaki (1998a, 131) makes an extended comment on Hisaishi's cue for this scene. In general, Miyazaki admired the "neutral nature" of what he calls Hisaishi's "minimal [minimalist] music" for Totoro that achieved a perfect balance between something that is unfamiliar but not overly mystical. Yet, while mixing the music for this episode—a process for which both Miyazaki and Hisaishi were present—Miyazaki found Hisaishi's music to be excessive and asked him to eliminate parts of it. Hisaishi readily agreed to do so, silencing and reinserting music he had already composed at regular intervals. To Miyazaki, the result was music that uncannily matched the pacing of the film. He praised the cue for "not interfering or determining the character [of Totoro], yet producing an odd and mysterious feeling that was nevertheless not extremely mysterious and strangely familiar."

While Mei's introduction to Totoro begins with cues derived from "My Neighbor Totoro," Satsuki's encounter with Totoro avoids any references to the tuneful image song. This unfamiliarity, in turn, adds to the mystery of Totoro appearing suddenly right next to (*tonari no*) Satsuki. It avoids the entrance of Totoro from becoming overly familiar, "as if a badger (*mujina*) has come out" (Miyazaki 1988, 131). The contrast also subtly differentiates the two sisters' relationship with Totoro. As discussed earlier, the instrumental presentation of "My Neighbor Totoro" at the end of Mei's scene with Totoro conveys a sense of safety which Mei immediately finds in Totoro. Satuski, who is older than Mei by several years, has not yet become completely at ease with Totoro, although she is considerate enough to lend Totoro her father's umbrella.

Hisaishi's cue only lasts a little over a minute and a half, yet the remainder of the scene is rich with the sounds of nature. First, Totoro reacts positively to the sound of water dripping off the tree branch. Then Totoro creates a minor tremor by jumping up and landing heavily on the ground, forcing the accumulated water on the trees to fall loudly in a torrent. Even more excited, Totoro emits a loud roar. The girls notice a pair of bright headlights approaching them. They think it is the bus that they have been waiting for so long, but it turns out to be a gigantic orange tabby with many legs, accompanied by the sound of the winds. Miyazaki and Hisaishi had originally planned to include a lively music cue but decided against it to maintain the mystery and the shock of the girls (Miyazaki 1988, 130). Before boarding the bus, Totoro hands Satsuki a small package made of bamboo leaves tied together with a strand of grass. As soon as it collects its customer, the Catbus dashes into the night, carrying Totoro still holding on to the umbrella. The rain has stopped, and the girls are left dumbstruck, until Satsuki finally utters "Totoro took Father's umbrella." As she has done before, Satsuki writes a letter to her mother about the content of the sac they received from Totoro. We learn that the girls planted the acorns that were in the small package. Every day, she writes, Mei sits in front of the small plot of land, waiting for the acorns to sprout. Hisaishi sets this heart-warming sequence [0:55:35] to an arrangement of another image song, "Mother" (I-8), discussed in Chapter 4.

Moonlit Flight

One hot moonlit summer night, sometime after the incident with the umbrella, Satsuki and Mei wake up to see the trio of Totoro engaged in a strange dance in the yard where they have planted the acorns. They go out to join in the strange ritual, and the acorns in the ground magically begin to sprout. Further efforts by Large Totoro turns the seedlings into saplings, and the saplings into small trees. To set the ambience for this scene [0:57:15], Hisaishi provides a musical cue that combines elements from "Totoro's Theme" and the drumbeats extracted from the image song "Dondoko Festival" (I-10) (see Chapter 5).

The cue here is particularly complex and disorienting one, because of the way Hisaishi layers cycles of repeating rhythmic patterns of different lengths. Pulsating chords on the synthesizer, melodic fragments on the marimba, and sustained pitches of synthesized organ and voices float over the regular *taiko* drumbeats of "Dondoko Festival." Although the trio of Totoro are engaged in regular rhythmic activity throughout the ritual, Hisaishi's music is not synchronized to the gestures of the creatures. In contrast to the music during Mei's chase of the Totoro, the loose relationship between the music and the image here creates a dream-like atmosphere. Hisaishi introduces another cue based on "The Path of the Wind" (I-2), when the sprouts grow into saplings, and the saplings combine themselves into a massive tree [0:58:44].

Once their work has been accomplished, Large Totoro takes out a top and spins it so that it hovers above the ground. The other Totoro jump on and cling to Large Totoro's chest, followed by Mei. Large Totoro jumps onto the top and invites, without speaking, a hesitant Satsuki to join the crowd. When Satsuki joins them, Totoro flies up into the branches above, bringing all of them to the top of the tree. Totoro and the girls fly high above the village, roar into the night sky, swoop down toward the surface, and glide just above the rice paddies, creating ripples among the rice stalks. The tune from "My Neighbor Totoro" makes another important entrance in this iconic moment representing the girls' magical adventure with Totoro [1:00:00].

The cue, again arranged by Hirabe, starts when Satsuki intuits Large Totoro's invitation and jumps onto his chest. (This cue is included on the track "Moonlit Flight" [Tsukiyo no hikō, S-15], starting at 1:04.) The music starts with an anticipatory ascending figure that leads into the Totoro refrain from "My Neighbor Totoro." Scored for full symphonic orchestra with prominent parts for trumpet and marimba, the music conveys the sense of excitement and joy. The chromatic harmonies that give the passage a sense of instability suggest the thrill felt by the sisters. As in so many other cues associated with Totoro, the music throughout is mixed together with the sound of the wind. The transition to the calmer and slightly melancholic verse section of the song coincides with the image of Totoro and the girls gliding over the rice paddies [1:00:42]. The lower strings carry the melody, and the orchestration thins out. Satsuki excitedly tells Mei that "we've turned into the wind."

The girls' father, busy at work in his study, remains completely oblivious to their adventure. As Satsuki had earlier, he does hear Totoro playing the Totoro refrain on the ocarina and tilts his head toward it in appreciation [1:01:08]. He also reacts with surprise and bemusement to the music of a less experienced player. This turns out to be Satsuki playing the ocarina perched among the trio of Totoro. Mei too blows on the ocarina but has a difficult time producing a good sound. The scene cuts to the following morning. The girls wake up and notice that the tree is gone. However, they see the seedlings that had sprouted overnight. They reenact their mysterious dance, chanting, "It was a dream, but it was *not* a dream," over a reprise of the final moments from the orchestrated verse of "My Neighbor Totoro" [1:02:07]. As promised in the song, a magical adventure did open up for the girls.

Totoro to the Rescue

Miyazaki's sketches from early in the process suggest that he had many ideas about the ways in which the girl (there was only one at this stage) interacted with the trio of Totoro: Satsuki/Mei fishing with the little Totoro, Satsuki/Mei and the giant Totoro overlooking a house with the *koinobori* streamers[3] (another nod to the month of May), Satsuki/Mei and the Totoro singing at the pond, etc. (Miyazaki 2005, 8–21). In the film, however, Miyazaki realizes only a few of these images. Nonetheless, the Totoro and the music associated with them make one crucial appearance during a climactic moment in the film—when Satsuki, riding the Catbus, comes to rescue Mei, who has gotten lost.

When Satsuki realizes that Mei had originally wanted to deliver an ear of corn to their mother, the Catbus changes its display from "Mei" to the "Shichikoku Yama Hospital." An instrumental cue based on "My Neighbor Totoro," included on the soundtrack album as "I'm So Glad" (Yokattane) (S-18), sneaks in at this point and accompanies the girls' fantastical bus ride [1:22:02]. The cue begins from the second half of the chorus starting with the Totoro refrain followed by the dramatic octave leap in the melody. The sudden swell of the full orchestra, with rapid scalar runs in the strings over an active rhythmic accompaniment, conveys the excitement and delight of the girls' journey on the Catbus. When the camera cuts to the scene in the hospital room where the girls' parents are having a conversation, the orchestration becomes more intimate [1:22:15]. A solo trumpet repeats the final phrase of the chorus over a gentle harp and string accompaniment. The string orchestra, with the addition of the harp, continues the verse of the song as the parents talk about their children. The camera cuts again to show the girls' point of view and then the girls perched on a pine tree with the Catbus. They can't hear what their parents are saying, but they can see that they are smiling and laughing. The music swells momentarily, with a more active accompaniment pattern in the lower strings that refers back to the music that accompanied Mei's nap on Large Totoro [1:22:53]. Even though Totoro is not seen on the screen, its warm presence is felt through Hisaishi's tender music.

Hisaishi pauses the music when the father sees an ear of corn left on the windowsill. As he looks out of the window, he wonders who left the mysterious gift. The mother also looks out and tells him that she felt the presence of the girls. The father agrees with her and shows her the ear of corn scratched with the message: "To Mommy" (Okāsan e). The instrumental introduction to "My Neighbor Totoro" begins while the camera lingers on the close-up of the ear of corn, signaling the conclusion of the film [1:23:37]. The finale of the film is a montage sequence depicting the conclusion of this adventurous day, accompanied by Inoue's performance of the ending theme song. The Catbus delivers the girls back to their home, and the girls have a tearful reunion with Granny and Kanta. They are seen talking, but we are no longer privy to their conversations. The camera cuts to show the four of them walking to the house next to the mound with the camphor tree. The final shot, before the ending credit sequence, shows the trio of Totoro atop the tree, playing the ocarina, with Large Totoro holding on to his black umbrella.

The image song, "My Neighbor Totoro," seamlessly bridges the final moments of the film with the ending credit sequence. This sequence is a series of still images, showing how the narrative continues over the remainder of the year. It shows the mother's arrival at the house in a taxi, followed by a series of images against a tangerine background, showing the girls with their mother and with children from the village. The trio of Totoro also appear celebrating various seasonal events, but they are never seen again with the girls. Various motifs from the film—acorns, Small Totoro, mushrooms, *susuwatari*, and ladybugs—adorn the upper and lower borders of each frame. Hisaishi introduces a slight but meaningful modification to the image song version of "My Neighbor Totoro" at the conclusion of the film: he cuts the instrumental interlude between the first chorus and the second verse. He also replaces the coda from the image song, the seemingly endless repetition of the Totoro refrain, with a newly composed musical passage that brings the piece to a definitive conclusion in the home key of F. Curiously, the version of the song included in the soundtrack album, "My Neighbor Totoro: Ending Theme Song" (S-19) does not include these changes. Now that their mother has come home, the family is complete.

* * *

To the uninitiated, *My Neighbor Totoro* is a surprisingly difficult film to describe. It starts out as a period drama that lovingly depicts the minute details of the ordinary life of a family who moved into a house in the Japanese countryside in the recent past: the three-wheeled moving van that the family travels in, the pump well at the back of the house, the bath operated by a burning-wood stove, the untended backyard of the house overgrown with tall weeds, and the sight of entire families crouched knee-deep, planting rice in the paddies. Even though many viewers may not have direct memories of objects and events depicted in the narrative, the amount of time and detail that Miyazaki and his animators spent in realizing, for example, the way Satsuki prepares breakfast for the family on her first day of school and Mei's excitement at her magical hand putting together their bento boxes, endow the film with a great sense of reality. At the same time, Miyazaki's imagination freely incorporates fantastical creatures in the otherwise naturalistically depicted world of the film. First, it was the mass of *susuwatari* (dust bunnies) that scurry away when Satsuki and Mei open the backdoor to the kitchen. Later that night, we see the *susuwatari* moving away from the house in the moonlight. Finally, a third of the way into the film, Mei encounters a pair of Totoro in the backyard, suddenly turning the film into something beyond a period film, but one that interlaces episodes of realism with fantasy.

The music that Hisaishi composed for the figure of Totoro represents this duality in sound. The image song, "My Neighbor Totoro"—composed in the spirit of *dōyō* but inflected with elements of minimalist and popular music— seems to represent Totoro as a familiar creature. It is the music that accompanies Mei's discovery of Small Totoro and Medium Totoro in broad daylight. On the other hand, the mysterious "Totoro's Theme" that wafts around the figure of Large Totoro clearly points to the otherworldly nature of that being. If "My Neighbor Totoro" reconciles the existence of Totoro within a familiar musical framework that invites us to sing along, the difficulty of describing "Totoro's Theme" reminds us of the challenge of truly understanding this being. Because the theme is presented in conjunction with the sounds of natural phenomena, it also teaches us to pay careful attention to the sounds of nature. Or perhaps it *reminds* us of a time when we thought we could comprehend the sounds that nature makes, like Satsuki and Mei do. Simultaneously familiar and unfamiliar, realistic yet fantastical, Hisaishi's music perfectly captures this duality of Totoro at the heart of Miyazaki's film.

4 The Wind and the Forest

"The Path of the Wind" (I-2) is one of three items on the *Image Song Collection* with lyrics written by Miyazaki. The image album includes two versions of the song: a texted version performed by the Suginami Children's Chorus and an instrumental version in which a metallic sound of the synthesizer replaces the children's voices (Example 4). Although the sung version of "The Path of the Wind" does not appear in the film, instrumental cues derived from the song permeate the soundtrack of *My Neighbor Totoro*, coinciding often with the presentation of the magnificent camphor tree at the top of the forested mound (*tsukamori*) next to Satsuki and Mei's house. Like the Totoro refrain discussed in Chapter 3, the melody functions as a leitmotif to signal the presence of the tree.[1] Arranged at times for acoustic instruments and at other times for electronic instruments, the varied and repeated presentations of the melody underscore the importance of the camphor tree within the narrative of the film. They also create a sense of cohesion in the film score, functioning very much like the film's "main theme" in the way Hisaishi conceives it, as discussed in Chapter 3. Perhaps because of this unifying quality, Hisaishi (1992, 69) calls "The Path of the Wind" "the hidden theme" [*ura tēma*] of *Totoro*.

Mo-ri no o-ku de u-ma - re-ta ka-ze ga ha-ra - p-pa ni hi-to-ri-ta-tsu ni - re no ki

Example 4 *"The Path of the Wind" (I-2, 0:16), the opening measures of the sung melody.*

The tune associated with the cue is quite memorable. Fans of *My Neighbor Totoro* often bring it up in conversations about its music, although many are surprised to hear that it was originally conceived as a song. Yet, although it is a highly recognizable piece, "The Path of the Wind" turns out to be tricky to describe. Many listeners note the tune's noticeably "Japanese," "Asian," or "Eastern" quality. This view is summarized by Japanese cultural historian Koizumi Kyoko's analysis, which points to Hisaishi's use of the *niroku-nuki* pentatonic scale in the melody of the song (C-E♭-F-G-B♭-C) (Example 5). *Niroku-nuki* can be translated to "pulling out two and six," meaning removing the second and sixth notes of a diatonic scale, in this case, the C minor scale.[2] According to Koizumi (2010, 68), Hisaishi's pentatonic melody matches the film's "Japanese-styled storyline" and contributes to its "tone of 'nostalgia.'"

However, Hisaishi (1992, 69) himself describes "The Path of the Wind" as having an "ethnic feel." As if to emphasize the tune's foreignness, Hisaishi uses the Japanese word *esunikku*, a transliteration for the English word "ethnic," rather than the more academic term *minzoku*. Hisaishi's word choice also connects the music to his "minimal and ethnic" style discussed in Chapter 2. This gap between the composer's recognition of the tune's non-Japaneseness and some audience members' perception of its Japaneseness encapsulates the challenge of any composer's original intent to be transmitted accurately

Example 5 Niroku-nuki *pentatonic scale based on the C minor scale.*

in a piece of music, or any artwork for that matter. The contemporaneous Japanese synthpop band, Yellow Magic Orchestra, famously played with the very notion of "otherness" to perform "an empty, parodic identity" back to the Western audience (Bourdaghs 2012, 188). This is especially true when a culturally specific animated film such as *Totoro* becomes popular outside of Japan. Yet, the recognition of this gap, I believe, actually makes our engagement with the film richer. The ability of "The Path of the Wind" to be perceived as both Japanese and *not* Japanese points to the composer's deliberate attempt at avoiding the soundtrack from becoming stereotypically "Japanese." The puzzling nature of Hisaishi's song, in turn, resonates with Miyazaki's own ambivalent, at times tortured, but ultimately positive attitude toward his own Japanese identity embodied in the film. After exploring the various elements of "The Path of the Wind" that point to Hisaishi's "minimal and ethnic" style, the chapter analyzes the narrative significances that the cues based on the song carry in the film and concludes with a discussion of Miyazaki's metaphorical "homecoming" in *My Neighbor Totoro*.

Image Song with an "Ethnic Feel"

When Hisaishi was asked whether he was conscious about the Japanese setting of the film while composing his music, he deflected the interviewer's question by sharing his personal and highly idiosyncratic view of Miyazaki's works.

> But [*My Neighbor Totoro*] is not rooted in the climate (*fūdo*) of Japan. I don't think Miyazaki-san's work has such specificity rooted in the climate (*fūdokan*). I was aware that *Totoro* is set in Japan, but I could not sense an indigenous atmosphere that can only be born in Japan (Hisaishi 1988 148).

Hisaishi's assessment of *My Neighbor Totoro* is striking because it seems to contradict Miyazaki's stated effort to create an entertaining work set in Japan that is rooted in his and his collaborators' lived experience (Miyazaki 1998a, 122). Following Miyazaki's cues, many commentators from Japan and elsewhere have interpreted the film in terms of its specifically Japanese environmental and cultural contexts (McDonald 2006; Odell and Le Blanc 2015; Greenberg, 2018; Napier 2018). Yet, as discussed earlier, Miyazaki himself was quite enthusiastic about Hisaishi's willingness to break away from traditional notions of Japanese music, an approach that can be observed in the image song, "The Path of the Wind."

In his autobiography, Hisaishi (1992, 68) discloses that the musical material for the song existed prior to his engagement with *Totoro*, suggesting a creative process similar to that discussed earlier for "My Neighbor Totoro," in which Miyazaki added lyrics to a melody composed by Hisaishi. However, unlike "My Neighbor Totoro," the text that Miyazaki wrote for "The Path of the Wind" does not engage directly with any character, scenery, or event from the film. Instead, Miyazaki's lyrics present a quiet, dream-like contemplation of the wind moving through an open landscape. The first stanza describes the journey of a wind that is born "in the depth of the forest" (*mori no oku de*). The wind passes through an open field, gently grazes a solitary elm tree, and approaches the speaker. Miyazaki personifies the wind in the second stanza, describing how it extends its invisible hand, lightly touching the wheat spikes and gently rustling "your hair" (*anata no kami*) before continuing its journey. After presenting two stanzas with the equal number of lines, Miyazaki inserts a shorter two-line stanza describing "your" lonely journey in the open landscape, comparing the wind to a signpost and an invisible hair ornament. The last stanza is almost identical to the first except here the wind disappears into nothingness instead of approaching the speaker. The landscape described in this poem also seem to be at odds with the image of the Japanese countryside depicted in *My Neighbor Totoro*. Instead of rice paddies, Shinto shrines, and old school buildings, the lyrics in "The Path of the Wind" present an unfamiliar scenery made up of a deep forest, open fields, a solitary elm tree, and wheat stalks. In adding words to Hisaishi's preexisting melody with an "ethnic feel," Miyazaki provided a text that depicts a strange but familiar imaginary scene.

As in "My Neighbor Totoro," the sung version of "The Path of the Wind" included on the *Image Song Collection* contains ample elements that can be described as "ethnic and minimal," especially in Hisaishi's choice of instrumental timbres and subtle rhythmic manipulation of the piece. The composer's nod to minimalism becomes immediately apparent in the introductory section of "The Path of the Wind." The introduction is made up of a repeating two-measure pattern with a sharp rhythmic profile played on a metallic synthesized sound. Hisaishi adds broken chords on the electric piano when the pattern is repeated for the second time and layers a steady sixteenth-note beat on the Linn drum on the third repetition. There is a little bit of a rhythmic *trompe-l'oeil* in this brief introduction. When you hear the music for the first time, it sounds as if the rhythmic pattern starts on the downbeat of the measure. However, when additional layers of music are superimposed, it becomes clear that the rhythmic pattern on the metallic synth sound actually started on an offbeat with a sixteenth-note rest. A close analysis of the recording also reveals that the two stereo tracks are offset from each other ever so slightly, by fifteen milliseconds, recreating the sensation of rhythmic ambiguity on a microscopic level. Hisaishi's interest in this kind of aural ambiguity dates back to his first encounter with minimalist music. Hisaishi's fascination with the idea of *trompe-l'oeil* continued through his later works including his 1985 solo album *α•BET•CITY* (1992, 216–17) and the music of *Totoro*.

A musical element that points to what I think Hisaishi means by the descriptor "ethnic" is the timbre of the composition. The timbre of the metallic riff discussed above is reminiscent of a pitched percussion instrument such as a glockenspiel or a vibraphone. Yet the sound is odd because it lacks the characteristic resonance of such instruments. The attack of the sound also has a wooden dull feel to it that is unusual for a metallic instrument. Repeated hearings also reveal that some of the pitches presented in this section sound slightly out of tune from each other to ears accustomed to the equal temperament commonly used in Western music. This combination of unusual timbre and unfamiliar tuning system contributes to the sense of the music being some-what foreign, evocative perhaps of Balinese gamelan, and, therefore, *esunikku* from his Japanese standpoint. This sense of uncertainty, however, adds to the attractiveness of the piece.

Hisaishi continues to play with our sense of expectations in the following measures. The harmonic accompaniment that enters in the third measure (0:06) not only clarifies the metric organization but also sets the tonal center of the piece in E♭ major. Hisaishi uses more familiar electric piano timbres for the harmonic accompaniment that provide unobtrusive background under the metallic riff. The steady beat of the Linn Drum in the last two measures of the introduction (0:11) adds an additional layer to this mix and contributes to the creation of excitement that leads up to the entrance of the children's chorus. The unique and recognizable timbre of children's voices, light, pure, and undifferentiated by gender, seems out of place in an album consisting of songs performed by adult singers. Yet the sound of children's voices is somewhat expected for a collection of songs modeled after *shōka* and *dōyō*. Another metallic sounding instrument doubles the children's choir while additional percussion instruments provide intricate rhythmic accompaniment. As the piece progresses, the solitary sound of the electric string instrument with a prominent vibrato joins in (0:18) and gradually comes to the foreground. The part provides a countermelody to the simple tune of the children's choir, and the tune becomes increasingly elaborate and even erratic, as if to illustrate in sound the path of the free-wheeling wind that blows across this unknown landscape described in Miyazaki's poem.

The Wind and the Forest in the Film

As stated earlier, the cues derived from this song are scattered throughout the first two-thirds of the film to indicate the presence of the camphor tree in key scenes: the Kusakabe family's farewell to the mover and Granny [0:18:07], the *susuwatari*'s migration to the camphor tree [0:20:42], at the start of the episode depicting Mei's first encounter with Totoro [0:25:11], at the end of Mei's chase for Totoro [0:31:28], the Kusakabe family's formal introduction to the camphor tree [0:38:41], and Satsuki and Mei's "magical adventure" with the trio of Totoro [0:58:44]. Hisaishi does not use the original sung version of "The Path of the Wind" included on the image album in the film but provides multiple arrangements using acoustic and synthesized sounds. These cues are gathered and included on the *Soundtrack Collection* as "The Evening Wind" (Yūgure no kaze, S-5), "I'm Not Scared" (Kowaku nai, S-6), "A Huge Tree on the Tsukamori" (Tsukamori no taiju, S-11), and "Moonlit Flight" (Tsukiyo no hikō, S-15). Although it does not appear on the actual soundtrack of the film, the *Soundtrack Collection* also includes the instrumental version of "The Path of the Wind" (S-13) from the *Image Song Collection*.

The first two presentations of the cues deriving from "The Path of the Wind" happen toward the end of the Kusakabe family's move-in day. The first cue appears when the Kusakabe family bids farewell to the mover and Granny [0:18:07]. It continues through the following sequence showing the family busy at their evening chores. The soundtrack presents an arrangement of the song on acoustic instruments, the English horn and the flute playing the doleful tune over a gentle string accompaniment at a tempo much slower than the song recorded on the image album. The presentation of the melody is subtle and understated. It uses familiar orchestral instruments that evoke the wistful mood at day's end. Throughout this sequence, however, Miyazaki arranges the shots in such a way that the camphor tree cannot be seen directly, obscuring the relationship between the music and the tree. Yet careful viewers of the film would understand, retrospectively, that the camphor tree has always been in the background. Our temporary "blindness" to the tree mirrors our cluelessness with regard to the spiritual significance of the camphor tree. At the same time, the introduction of the music played on familiar instruments and presented as a paraphrase of a familiar song gives us a sense of recognition regarding this scene.

The second cue deriving from the song appears minutes later to accompany the migration of the fuzzy black balls called *susuwatari*, establishing the melody's association with the camphor tree. While the family is engaged in a manic laughing contest in the bathtub, the camera shows the *susuwatari* streaming out of a corner of the ceiling in a single file toward an opening in the outer wall. The *susuwatari* float over a neatly arranged row of sundry items stored above the cabinet. The juxtaposition of the domestic interior and the oddity of the situation is enhanced by Hisaishi's music derived from the image song "Susuwatari" consisting of synthesized sounds and sampled voices (more on this song in Chapter 6). Midway through the sequence, as the *susuwatari* force themselves into a narrow corner of the house and waft into the moonlit night sky, Hisaishi overlays another instrumental arrangement of "The Path of the Wind" [0:20:42]. For this arrangement of the image song, Hisaishi uses the synthesizer rather than conventional orchestral instruments. The music continues as the *susuwatari* float toward the top of the camphor tree. The ethereal manner in which the *susuwatari* move in contrast to the more familiar motions of the clouds as well as the unusual sounds of the synthesizer playing a familiar melody add to the feeling that we are witnessing something magical and extraordinary. Together, the image and the music convey the transition from the ordinary to the extraordinary, from realism to fantasy. Furthermore, Hisaishi's presentation of the two contrasting arrangements of theme in close proximity alerts us to the dual nature of the camphor tree.

Like the first two examples, the next three cues based on "The Path of the Wind" also come in close succession to each other during Mei's first encounter with Totoro. The episode starts with a fade-in from a black screen showing the top of the camphor tree basked in the bright morning sun and a new cue based on "The Path of the Wind" arranged for the synthesizer [0:25:11]. The cue continues as the camera pans diagonally left from the top of the tree to the Kusakabe family's house at the base of the mound. The presentation of the tree and the house side by side demonstrates the physical and proportional relationship, the tree dwarfing the house. When the scene moves to the interior of the house, Hisaishi presents an unrelated, newly composed cue to show Satsuki opening the wooden shutters (*amado*) and calling loudly to her father to wake up. This rather nondescript, Muzak-like cue for the interior scene has the effect of enhancing the mystery and majesty of "The Path of the Wind" and the camphor tree associated with it.

The presentation of the theme here presages the appearance of Totoro, who lives inside the tree, later in the episode. Indeed, the Kusakabe family's morning routine leads to Mei's discovery and chase of Small Totoro and Medium Totoro (Chapter 3).

The melody of "The Path of the Wind" makes its fourth appearance at the end of this chase, when the pair of Totoro and Mei reach the camphor tree at the top of the hill [0:31:28]. Up until this point in the chase, Hisaishi strings together short snippets of music accompanying Mei's every gesture and expression in the style of Hollywood cartoons. The musical pacing, however, experiences a sudden shift when the camera shows the canopy of the camphor tree from below. The camera pans down to show the thick trunk of the tree and its gnarly roots. The English horn and the flute state the melody of the tune in a slightly modified form as the pair of Totoro and Mei scurry across the surface of the mossy tree. Even though it is light outside, the immediate surroundings of the tree are quite dark, giving a mysterious feel. As if to emphasize the majesty and the rootedness of the camphor tree, Miyazaki uses a long take to depict a moment that lasts about forty seconds.

The fifth cue based on "The Path of the Wind" takes place toward the conclusion of this episode after Mei's encounter with Large Totoro in its lair. Once Satsuki returns from school, Satsuki and her father look for Mei, who is discovered sleeping inside the hedge in the backyard. Mei wakes up from her slumber and explains her adventures to her sister and her father. She even tries to return to Totoro's lair but to no avail. When she senses that her sister and father are not taking her seriously, she starts to tear up. Seeing that his daughter is upset, her father quickly explains that Mei must have met the "lord of the forest" (*mori no nushi*). Suddenly he announces that he and his daughters have to pay a visit to this being. Instead of the secret passage that Mei took to meet Totoro, the father takes the family out the gate of the house, through the *torii* at the base of the mound marking the entrance to the Shinto shrine, and up the steep stone steps to the rustic and dilapidated miniature shrine (*hokora*) at the base of the camphor tree.

The cue starts quietly with a synth statement of the verse melody when the girls' father begins to talk to Mei, acknowledging her experience [0:38:41]. Hisaishi inserts a newly composed brief interlude, which is followed by another instrumental arrangement of "The Path of the Wind" using the synthesizer. The camera presents the exterior view of the house in an extreme long shot and moves to the right to show the entrance to the mountain shrine and the family climbing the steep stairs. The visual motion from left to right reverses the direction that the camera took at the beginning of the episode discussed above. The cue is arranged so that the restatement of the verse melody, following the introduction, coincides with the visual presentation of the tree. As before, the camera captures the canopy of the tree from below and moves downward to show the trunk and the roots. The tree looks different, however. The light has changed since we first saw the tree, and the tree looks brighter. However, the tree trunk seems somewhat shorter than it was before. Mei runs toward the backside of the tree but cannot find the entrance to the lair. The girls are disappointed, but the father assures them that they will see the Totoro once again if they are lucky. He turns his face toward the branches and expresses his admiration for the tree. He concludes the visit by leading a formal introduction, asking the tree to take care of the family, and a bow, which the girls mimic. The camera switches to show the family from above as if we are witnessing the scene from Totoro's point of view. The synth rendition of "The Path of the Wind" continues through this brief monologue and ends right before the family bow before the tree.

The sixth and final appearance of "The Path of the Wind" comes during the episode in which the sisters help the trio of Totoro in their life-giving ritual of the *dondoko* festival. While Hisaishi provides a different musical cue during the first half of the ritual, once the saplings begin to grow tall and merge together to form one gigantic tree, a triumphant arrangement of "The Path of the Wind" emerges [0:58:44]. The music, lasting for about fifty seconds, progresses unimpeded by any dialogue. We are compelled to look at, admire, and be awed by the sight of the growing tree. The musical arrangement here is an unusual combination of synthesized sounds adorned with orchestral embellishments. A brass fanfare introduces the synthesizer melody and the undulating string passages that envelop it. Combining the acoustic (orchestral sound) and the electronic (synthesized sound), the cue supports this dream-like scene that seems to defy logic. The tree eventually grows much taller. The music becomes momentarily softer here, and the girls' father, working late into the night, perceives that something extraordinary has happened. But he quickly returns to his work. The music concludes as the camera shows the girls standing with Totoro from above, a camera angle that mirrors that of the closing moment in the scene in which the family paid a visit to the camphor tree. Although we are dealing with two different trees, these parallels in the visual and sonic signs point to the duality of the camphor tree. While the previous scene takes place in broad daylight, this scene is covered in the steely blue light of the moon, suggesting that we have entered into the world of dream and magic.

At Home among Trees

Such a tall tree! It must have been standing here for a long, *long* time. Once upon a time, trees and humans were good friends. I became really fond of that house when I saw this tree. I thought to myself that your mother will also like it for sure.

Satsuki and Mei's father makes this statement while looking up toward the tall branches of the tree encouraging his daughters to do the same. The comment also anticipates the girls' friendship with the tree manifested in the form of Totoro. However, it is perhaps one of the few moments in the film where Miyazaki breaks the proverbial fourth wall and talks directly to the audience, reminding us of the bonds he believes that humans once had with nature. This call toward the recovery of the lost tie between humans and nature is one of the central themes that binds *My Neighbor Totoro* with many other films by Miyazaki, including *Nausicaä of the Valley of the Wind*, *Princess Mononoke*, and *Spirited Away*. However, the scene has a striking parallel to a moment from Miyazaki's life that he recounts in several interviews and essays he produced around the time of *My Neighbor Totoro*: the eye-opening "encounter" with Nakao Sasuke's book, *The Origins of Cultivated Plants and Agriculture* (1966) that enabled him to view Japanese nature in a brand new light and altered the way he felt about his identity as a Japanese person.

Scholars of Japanese history and culture such as Julie Adeney Thomas (2001) and Tessa Morris-Suzuki (2013) remind us that the oft-proclaimed Japanese love for nature is a product of a confluence of complex historical processes that binds environmentalism with nationalism in modern Japan. Furthermore, the publication of Nakao's books coincides with the rise of popular books in Japan that engage with *nihonjinron*, or the theory of Japan or Japanese (Befu 2001). A careful consideration of Miyazaki's brand of environmentalism should situate it within this larger context, which is beyond the scope of this book. For the limited purpose of this chapter, which is to consider the narrative implication of "The Path of the Wind" in *My Neighbor Totoro*, I now turn to a close reading of Miyazaki's writings about the impact of Nakao's book on his outlook on nature in Japan.

When recalling his first encounter with Nakao's book, Miyazaki uses the word "liberation" (*kaihō*) to express his reaction to its revelatory ideas. In one essay he calls this a "liberation from a curse" (*jubaku kara no kaihō*) (1996, 265) and in another he calls it a liberation from the "feeling of suffocation" (*heisokukan*) (1988, 126). According to his own writings, this "curse" for Miyazaki (1996, 266) was the internal conflict he experienced growing up into a "Japanese boy who hated Japan." Miyazaki (1988, 126), who was four years old when the Pacific War ended, recalls spending his formative years during the period of intense self-examination in Japanese society that tended to deny all things Japanese in an effort to embrace the new postwar democratic order and to reject its wartime militarism. He grew up listening to adults around him self-deprecate themselves as "fourth-class citizens," paint

Japanese history as a history of oppression and exploitation, and even problematize traditional village life as a "hotbed of poverty, ignorance, and ignorance of human rights" (Miyazaki 1996, 265). At the same time, he interacted with members of his extended family who remained unrepentant of their own actions during the war, including relatives who boasted about murdering Chinese people (Miyazaki 1996, 239 and 266). His own father, whose family business profited from wartime industry making parts for planes, remained nonchalant about his collaboration with the Japanese authority during the war (Miyazaki 1996, 239 and 266). By the time Miyazaki (1996, 239) entered Gakushūin University in 1959, he was tormented by the sense of guilt that seemed to have skipped his father and relatives, questioning his own existence as a product of a series of grave "mistakes" committed by his own family.

The "curse" continued into Miyazaki's early adulthood casting a dark shadow over the mind of the future director. As a professional animator, his dislike of things Japanese motivated him to create works set in foreign countries or based on subject matter from foreign sources (Miyazaki 1996, 266). One such project was the adaptation of Astrid Lindgren's children's book series *Pippi Longstocking*, which, although it did not come to fruition, took Miyazaki on his first overseas trip to Sweden in 1971. Two years later, Miyazaki (1996, 266) visited Switzerland in preparation for the animation series *Heidi, the Girl of Alps* (1974) and then to Argentina (2013, 274). These journeys that took Miyazaki outside of Japan, a homeland which he could not come to love, ironically, exasperated his inner conflict, as he was, at every turn, reminded of his Japaneseness. Miyazaki continued to experience the internal struggle of the emotional cost of coming to terms with his Japanese identity. Yet he recognized in himself a desire to affirm something, to overturn the overwhelming and suffocating feeling of having to define one's being through the exhausting process of negation. Such was the power of the curse.

This negation began to change when he was in his thirties as he came to recognize the natural beauty of Japanese trees and forests.[3] His fascination with domestic plants grew as he realized how unmoved he had been by the natural landscapes, especially trees, that he encountered during his sojourns in Sweden and Switzerland. Even though Miyazaki (1988, 126) could appreciate their beauty, they were unable to inspire the kind of fondness he began to feel toward the trees and forests he strolled through for leisure in Japan. The key to understanding this feeling, Miyazaki later recalls, was in Nakao's book. Nakao claims that the inhabitants of the Japanese archipelago belong to a larger group of people who share some customs and inhabit a particular climatic region that stretches from the Eastern Himalayas (Bhutan) to Southern China (Yunnan Province) to Western Japan. This was a crucial discovery, a "liberation," that enabled Miyazaki (1988, 126; 1996, 267) to affirm his own identity positively, as a person rooted in the land in which he grew up. Nakao's theory enabled Miyazaki (1988, 126) to acknowledge being a descendant of a people belonging to a common culture without limiting his membership to the Japanese nation-state, whose problematic history of warfare and exploitation he continued to question, or promoting the officially sanctioned products and practices of Japanese culture that to him seemed removed and sterile. This moment of realization liberated Miyazaki from the curse.

Although Nakao's book was published in 1966 when Miyazaki was fifteen years old, the director makes a special note of saying that he was in his thirties when Nakao started to unfold his idiosyncratic theory (Miyazaki 1988, 126). This inconsistency may simply mean that it took some time for Miyazaki to become aware of Nakao's book, and that he was, indeed, in his early thirties when he first read it. However, it is also interesting to note that this puts Miyazaki around the same age as Satsuki and Mei's father in the movie, at least in the initial plans of the film seen on one of the sketches (Miyazaki 2005, 50). Miyazaki projects his own interests and understanding of Japanese history and Japanese culture onto the figure of the father in other ways as well. Little is explained in the film about the father's occupation, but through Satsuki we know that he works in the archaeology department at a university in Tokyo. We also have a glimpse of him working at home in the library facing a manuscript surrounded by piles of books. In one shot, the camera captures a spine of a book with the title *Forest and Agriculture* (*Mori to nōkō*) reminiscent of the title of Nakao's book. On the wall behind him, there is a framed image of what appears to be an ornate pottery from the prehistoric *jōmon* era. This reference to prehistoric Japan subtly betrays Miyazaki's homage to another one of his favorite historians, Fujimori Eiichi, who wrote about the riches of *jōmon*-era culture and promoted an unconventional theory about the beginning of agriculture in Japan (Miyazaki 1996, 265–67). These clues suggest that the father is a writer/historian like those Miyazaki admired.

* * *

The postwar period saw Japanese intellectuals engaged in the dismantling of antiquated ideologies as well as in painful acts of self-examination. However, the onset of rapid economic prosperity, political and social stability, and intermittent bursts of anti-government or anti-US student movements, brought about the re-evaluation of traditional Japanese values. Typical of the generation of Japanese who came of age in this environment, Miyazaki grew up with conflicting attitudes toward Japan's historic and cultural accomplishments as well as his own identity as a Japanese individual. However, Miyazaki had a moment of clarity in his adulthood when he began to appreciate what he felt to be his instinctive attachment to the lush, green vegetation of Japan. Nostalgic for a place where he could truly feel at ease, Miyazaki finally found himself at home among the familiar trees in the forests of Japan. Miyazaki thematizes this special sense of homecoming in the Kusakabe family's relationship with the camphor tree. Hisaishi provides these moments in the film with a cue based on "The Path of the Winds" that also explores the challenges of finding one's home in modern Japan through music that is familiar yet unfamiliar, Japanese yet *esunikku*.

5 Satsuki and Mei

While Hisaishi composed multiple pieces of music to describe the figure of Totoro in sound and music, he did not compose any themes representing Satsuki or Mei, the two sisters at the center of the film. Instead, Hisaishi composed a series of instrumental cues for the film soundtrack that illustrates the sisters' actions and sentiments. The *Soundtrack Collection* includes pieces that are clearly related to these cues but not exactly as they appear on the film soundtrack. These are "A Haunted House!" (Obake yashiki, S-3), "Mei and the Susuwatari" (Mei to Susuwatari, S-4), "Mother" (Okāsan, S-8), and "A Lost Child" (Maigo, S-12). To make things even more complicated, three of these tracks, "Mei and the Susuwatari," "Mother," and "A Lost Child," are based on preexisting compositions, three songs from the *Image Song Collection*, with similar or identical titles, "Susuwatari" (I-5), "Mother" (I-8), and "A Lost Child" (I-4). One of the goals of this chapter is to take note of the different strategies Hisaishi employed for composing the soundtrack for *My Neighbor Totoro*, revealing the extent to which the composer and the film director collaborated in the process of making the film's soundtrack.

Another goal of the chapter is to cast a different light on the meanings of Satsuki and Mei's adventures by considering the lyrical and musical contents of these three image songs.

Collectively, Hisaishi's image songs and cues emphasize the fragility of Satsuki and Mei's sense of happiness and security. In the film, moments of joy that the sisters share with each other can swiftly turn into episodes of anxiety. At the basis of this tension is the sisters' shared fear of abandonment triggered by their mother's illness and absence. This absence points to a specific form of nostalgia the girls experience. Even though the film's opening sequence was deliberately designed to elicit nostalgic reactions from the older Japanese viewers, the sisters themselves are never seen feeling homesick for their house or friends they presumably had left in Tokyo. This is not to say, however, that Satsuki and Mei lack the sense of yearning characteristic of the condition of nostalgia. What they long for is not a house in a place they left behind but the return of their mother into their household, the reconstitution of the family in one place. The film then provides yet another interpretation of nostalgia as a longing to be reunited with one's mother.[1]

"A Haunted House" (S-3)

Satsuki and Mei climb out of the back of the moving truck as soon as it makes a stop just outside the gate of their new house. The sisters are immediately distracted by the sound of the clear stream that flows just outside the entrance and the little fish swimming in it. When their father starts unloading a couple of items from the truck, their attention shifts quickly to the house at the top of the small incline through the narrow passageway flanked by shady trees. Satsuki dashes through what she excitedly calls "the tunnel of trees" and beholds the curious-looking house, followed closely by Mei who mimics her big sister's every word and action. Here begins the sisters' joyous exploration of their new house.

Hisaishi conveys Satsuki and Mei's excitement with a jaunty instrumental cue that starts as soon as the sisters' attention shifts from the brook to the house [0:4:51]. It starts with a brief introduction followed by a cheerful theme made up of two independent instrumental voices that play the same melody in imitation, or one part following the other with a slight delay (Example 6). The cue does not follow the actions of the sisters precisely in the style of mickey-mousing. However, its imitative musical structure mirrors how Mei closely follows her sister's words and actions.

Once the girls get closer to the house, the camera shows what they see: the partially rotten wooden trellis, the discolored sidings of the house, the small piles of dead leaves on the patio, and the gutters above the closed shutters that are bent out of shape. Satsuki's first impression of the house is that it is "*boro*" (worn out, falling apart), an opinion quickly echoed by Mei. Satsuki quickly elaborates that the house actually looks like "a haunted house!" (*obake yashiki*, literally "monster manor"). Mei, who cannot quite understand or say the word "manor," yells out "monster!?" Hisaishi repeats the melody several times, exploring different combinations of

Example 6 *"A Haunted House" (S-3), the opening measures.*

woodwind and string timbres on the synthesizer, and adding different layers of repeating rhythmic patterns to depict the sisters' mounting excitement. The cue fades away, however, when Satsuki swings around one of the pillars of the trellis and realizes that it is falling apart. The girls become momentarily concerned but they continue their cheerful exploration, scampering around the yard, laughing out loud, until Satsuki becomes aware of the tall tree behind their backyard.

Hisaishi's cue in this sequence of events is reproduced on the *Soundtrack Collection* as the track, "A Haunted House!" (S-3). The track on the album, however, also includes an arrangement of "The Path of the Wind," featuring futuristic bell-like timbres that contrast with the more familiar sounds in the first half of the track (1:04). There is no direct information about the creation of this cue in the sources I consulted, but, based on what we know about the nature of Miyazaki and Hisaishi's collaboration, we can reasonably assume that this track in the *Soundtrack Collection* represents the original version of the cue from the planning stage after the completion of the *Image Song Collection*. Indeed, the timing of "The Path of the Wind" on the track corresponds with the visual presentation of the camphor tree in the film, suggesting that the second half of the cue was to function as the first appearance of the so-called "hidden theme." For some reason, this part of the cue was edited out completely, perhaps during the mixing stage, so that the leitmotif of the camphor tree does not appear at this point in the film.

The suppression of "The Path of the Wind" from this cue, however, makes dramatic sense. In the film, the musical cue for "A Haunted House" stops when Satsuki leans against the pillar of the rotting trellis. Ending the cue at this point highlights this sudden shift in Satsuki's mood. Musical silence also enables the ensuing laughter and excited dialog between the two girls to ring out louder. In this film, moments of musical silence bring out important dialogs and ambient sounds, creating dramatic tensions. The subtle ambient sounds of rustling trees and chirping birds—the sounds of nature—also come to the fore as the girls focus their attention on the camphor tree. Finally, the presentation of the camphor tree as primarily a visual object stresses its everyday quality. Including the mystical sounds of "The Path of the Wind" at this point in the film would have signaled something magical and extraordinary about the tree. The magic of Totoro is, after all, something the girls can only discover by focusing their minds on and paying close attention to their surroundings.

Once the father identifies the tree for Satsuki and Mei, the girls continue their exploration, this time in the interior of the house. In the process, they discover acorns and encounter the hoard of fuzzy black balls with googly eyes in the kitchen—the first real sign of something strange about the house. When the girls report back to their father, he gives his daughters a quasi-scientific explanation of what they had just seen. What they saw, according to him, was the *makkuro kurosuke*, a temporary blinding that happens whenever entering a dark place from a bright place. The girls sing a short song and quickly turn their attention to their new task: finding the staircase to the second floor. After a long musical pause lasting about four and a half minutes, a new cue enters to accompany the girls chasing each other as they explore different corners of the house in search of the elusive staircase [0:10:00]. The cue is almost identical to the previous one, with the introduction and the ending trimmed to fit the scene. The elaborate camerawork seems to be designed to highlight the layout of the house and the fluid way in which one can move from one space to another in a traditional Japanese house divided by sliding doors and screens. Again, the jaunty mood of the music, as well as its imitative texture, mirror the events on the screen without tight synchronization between the music and action. The music, however, comes to a halt when Satsuki finds and opens the door to the stairway to the attic. The girls have now entered a new stage of their exploration, centering on their confrontation with the *makkuro kurosuke* accompanied by a different cluster of cues.

"Mei and the Susuwatari" (S-4)

What the girls see when Satsuki opens the door is a narrow and steep staircase that leads up into a dark void. Satsuki catches a small acorn that tumbles down from above, as if it were a mysterious invitation for them to climb up the stairs. The girls scream at the bottom of the stairs for the *makkuro kurosuke* to come out. They hear more rustling sounds, but seeing nothing happening, they gingerly climb up the stairs and yell at the top of their lungs once they poke their heads into a dark, dusty, empty attic. When Satsuki calls out to the *makkuro kurosuke-san* in a politer tone, several fuzzy black balls swoosh behind her. Up until this point, the presence of the *makkuro kurosuke* has only been accompanied by the sound effect suggestive of the rustling of dried leaves or, perhaps more grotesquely, the sound of a large group of insects scattering across the floor. Here, however, Hisaishi combines the rustling sound effect with a brief cue, consisting of woodwind instruments playing a series of rapid passages up and down the whole-tone scale [0:12:02]. Although extremely brief—it lasts only for about five seconds—the cue conveys a sense of wonder and excitement.

Spooked by the strange presence of the creatures, Satsuki runs forward to open the window on the opposite wall. When Mei stands up to follow her, she hears and then sees a large hoard of fuzzy black balls fly out from a corner of the room and disappear into a crack in the wall. While Satsuki runs down to help her father, Mei focuses her attention on the crack where she sees strange shadows wavering. Ever the intrepid adventurer, Mei carefully approaches the wall and pokes her finger into the opening. Suddenly a large group of fuzzy black balls spews out of the crack to escape her inquisitive digit and rushes up into a corner of the ceiling. Hisaishi repeats the brief musical cue but with a more extensive symphonic orchestration playing at full volume to convey the enormity of the crisis [0:13:06]. A single ball fails to escape and leisurely falls toward the ground. Hisaishi's cue continues with a thinner orchestration, playing new musical materials. Mei opens her arms wide as the music swells and slaps her hand capturing the fuzzy ball with a loud orchestral bang [0:13:27]. This is another clear instance of Hisaishi using the mickey-mousing technique that endows the scene with a familiar, cartoon-like mood.

Now that she has captured the *makkuro kurosuke*, Mei excitedly rushes down the stairs to show it to her sister. Hisaishi switches to another cue derived from "A Haunted House" to convey Mei's excitement tinged with uncertainty about what to do with the creature between her hands [0:13:28]. When she reaches the bottom of the stairs, she bumps into an unfamiliar old woman. Mei, surprised by the appearance of a stranger, continues to run around the house. Several large boxes and packages now occupy the formerly empty living room and the house suddenly seems crowded. Although referring back to "A Haunted House," the quality of the music that had accompanied the sisters' carefree exploration of the house seems to have changed too. Hisaishi layers the jaunty theme from "A Haunted House" with loud explosive chords or "stinger chords" that punctuate the texture at irregular intervals. The hectic pace of the music now seems to highlight Mei's panic and confused state of mind instead of the joy of discovery. The cue eventually dies down when Mei manages to hide behind Satsuki and looks to the older woman with curiosity and suspicion.

When Satsuki recounts the small adventure she and her sister had in the attic, Granny explains that what the girls saw were the *susuwatari* that "bubble up" in empty houses and make everything sooty and dusty. Granny's imaginative and curious explanation contrasts with the one the father had offered earlier in the film. (Here, too, Miyazaki points out two ways of seeing and understanding the world.) The father asks Granny if the soot sprites were *yōkai*, referring to supernatural beings or monsters in Japanese folklore (Foster 2015). The father's question suggests his interest in the local folklore, giving a subtle hint about his occupation and intellectual proclivities. Granny gently reassures him and the girls that the *susuwatari* are nothing scary like that. As long as they remain cheerful, she says, the *susuwatari* will do no harm and disappear one day. Granny then continues that the *susuwatari* must be having a meeting up in the attic, debating whether to move out from the house or not.

The camera momentarily shifts to the scene of the *susuwatari* gathering in the corner of the attic around a Shinto talisman, an open paper fan, painted with a pair of cranes around the sun, tied to a stick decorated with strips of red and white paper and yellow cords [0:15:31]. Hisaishi introduces a miniature musical cue, lasting only three seconds, to coincide with the "meeting" of the *susuwatari* in the attic. The cue consists of incomprehensible vocal utterances, maracas-like sounds, and a two-note upward gesture outlining a minor seventh on a plucked string instrument. Because of the cue's extreme brevity and unusual timbral profile, we might be inclined to perceive it as a sound effect rather than a piece of music. It is not clear whether the image and the music are meant to depict an event actually happening in the attic or something that the characters are imagining in their heads. Miyazaki leaves such ambiguities in the film unanswered, suggesting the possibility of multiple interpretations, similar to the two interpretations of the *susuwatari* presented by the father and Granny.

Hisaishi introduces a total of four cues to accompany the girls' interactions with the *susuwatari*, all related to a single track on the *Soundtrack Collection*, "Mei and Susuwatari" (S-4). The track itself is made up of multiple musical ideas that combine existing as well as newly composed materials; however, the order in which Hisaishi presents his ideas in the track differs from the way the cues are deployed in the film. The track opens with an instrumental version of the image song "Susuwatari" (I-5) that lasts for forty seconds. Even though this musical idea is presented first in the track, in the film, it returns at the end of the sequence, as the three-second cue that accompanies the *susuwatari* debating their future in the attic. "Mei and the Susuwatari" then makes a sudden shift to the full orchestral version of the whole-tone passage that accompanies Mei's poking her finger into the crack, depicting the panicked hoard of *susuwatari*. This panic music leads smoothly to the comedic passage that accompanies the single *susuwatari*'s futile effort to escape Mei's clutches, her eventual victory punctuated with a loud crash. The track concludes with the music that recycles parts of "A Haunted House," depicting Mei's own panicked escape from Granny.

Assuming again that the track included on the soundtrack album represents the initial version of the cue proposed by Hisaishi, comparing the track "Mei and the Susuwatari" and the actual cues in the film suggests a rather complicated process of editing and recomposing during the planning and mixing stages of the score. For instance, the very first cue in this sequence of events, the five-second, whole-tone, solo-woodwind passage that accompanies the *susuwatari*'s movement in the top of the attic turns out to be derived from the full orchestral statement of the panic music. Furthermore, had Miyazaki decided to make full use of the track as Hisaishi originally conceived, the first section of the track based on "Susuwatari" could have accompanied the image of dark shadows that wiggle in the corner of the room, presented immediately before Mei sticks her finger into the crack. However, like the suppression of "The Path of the Wind" during the sisters' exploration of their new haunted house, the elimination of "Susuwatari" makes dramatic sense in that the presence of the music would have contributed negatively to the building up of tension at this point in the narrative.

Hisaishi's song "Susuwatari" from the *Image Song Collection,* with lyrics by Nakagawa, is an oddly humorous but perplexing piece of music that warrants some discussion. The song opens with an intricate, highly syncopated rhythmic groove featuring unpitched percussion instruments, most likely a shaker and a pair of drums, giving it a distinct Latin or Afro-Caribbean feel. This focus on the rhythm immediately recalls Hisaishi's earlier minimalist compositions included in the album *Mkwaju* (1981), which freely combines West African drumming patterns with Latin percussion instruments and synthesized sounds. After establishing the groove, Hisaishi introduces a series of vocal utterances that sound unnaturally high. In an interview, Hisaishi (1988, 149) reveals that this effect was created by sampling and manipulating the voices of people from "the pygmy tribe in Africa." Hisaishi claimed to have sampled only a brief snippet, the sound "a," for this purpose. With this material, he creates a series of nonsensical vocal utterances that adds to the odd but strangely disarming mood of the introduction. This introduction prepares the entrance of the Suginami Children's Chorus, singing Nakagawa's poem set to Hisaishi's melody.

This poem also matches the absurdist mood of the introduction. Written in the "simple and straightforward poetic style" that Hisaishi found so challenging to set, a large portion of Nakagawa's poem is devoted to the repetition

Example 7 *"Susuwatari" (I-5, 0:15), the opening measures of the sung melody.*

of the syllable "su" that almost always precedes the word "susuwatari." The first line of the song, for instance, is "Sūsusu susuwatari" (Example 7). The overall sense of the creatures is that they are happy-go-lucky beings that float and wander around without any particular aim. Hisaishi's melody for the song is angular with repetitive and predictable rhythmic patterns. The use of a major key (G major), moderately fast tempo, and the decorative runs on synthesized woodwind instruments all contribute to creating a lighthearted song that sounds deliberately childlike. "Susuwatari" also has a relatively slow harmonic rhythm (rate at which the chords change), representing the permanent presence of the *susuwatari* in old houses. In the final four measures of the verse (there are three verses), however, Hisaishi introduces a chromatically inflected descending bass line that increases the harmonic rhythm and propels the music toward its conclusion. After setting two verses of Nakagawa's poetry to the same melody, Hisaishi suddenly modulates the music up by a half step, a trick he uses in other songs on the album. The piece concludes with the rhythmic groove of the shaker that opened the song.

The mysterious vocal utterances from the introduction punctuate the song at regular intervals, often right before the entrances of the children's chorus. In the context of the song and the film, these voices can be understood to represent the *susuwatari*'s collective voice. It is as if the *susuwatari* are giving the children's chorus brief words of encouragement, or *kakegoe*, resembling the call-and-response performing practice observed in Japanese folk music (*minyō*) (Hughes 2008, 30–31). Freely mixing elements of minimalism, Latin percussion, voices of the pygmy peoples, and Japanese folk music, Hisaishi creates a charming and humorous song, "Susuwatari." The song itself makes a minimal appearance in the film, only heard in one fleeting moment when the *susuwatari* are seen debating whether to vacate the house they have lived in for a long time.

The voices of the pygmy people play an important role in the song; however, the musicians are not recognized on the cover or the liner notes of the image album or the soundtrack album. In his monograph on reggae music and Rastafarianism in Japan, Marvin D. Sterling (2010, 27) points out that the Japanese people's adaptation of Jamaican popular culture, even though they may be sincere, is made possible "through structural racisms which facilitate the first world's gazing at, and taking from, black people with little need for concern about black opinion." Even though Hisaishi did seriously engage with musical traditions from West Africa (1992, 198) and befriended an ethnomusicologist from Mali (2006, 148), Hisaishi's access to technology that enabled him to manipulate the music of the pygmy people at his will reflects a similar situation. The connection that Hisaishi makes between the voices of the pygmy people and the *susuwatari*, whose primarily physical attributes are their diminutive size and darkness, is perhaps a questionable element in Hisaishi's music for *My Neighbor Totoro*.

Visiting Mother

The next cluster of cues centering on the sisters' actions takes place sometime shortly after the family's move. On one sunny day, the father takes his daughters on a trip to visit their mother at the hospital. The journey is depicted in a montage sequence that lasts for about a minute and a half, set to an instrumental arrangement of the image song "Hey Let's Go" [0:21:31]. The cue is included in the soundtrack album as "Let's Go to the Hospital" (Omimai ni ikō, S-7). The sequence depicts the bucolic landscape of the village, where entire families are working in the paddies planting rice. This display of the villagers at work situates the Kusakabe family as outsiders. In fact, Satsuki is able to visit her mother precisely because her school is on a "rice planting break." Kanta and many other classmates of Satsuki work in the field alongside their parents. Featuring the synthesized sounds of woodwind and brass instruments over the steady beat of the snare drum, the cue presents one complete verse of the song and then modulates up by a half step to repeat the verse. It stops, however, before reaching its conclusion when the camera pans to show the view of a group of buildings nestled among pine trees.

The cue here is slightly ironic since the family members ride the single bicycle while the music calls out for the children to walk. Yet, in a brief montage sequence, the cheerful mood of the song matches perfectly the optimism and excitement of the girls as they travel through the landscape dotted with landmarks similar to those listed in Nakagawa's poem (a grassy field, a bridge, an upward hill, etc.). Even the melodically and harmonically inconclusive ending of the cue helps the narrative to move smoothly from the family's travel to the following sequence.

The music ceases when the family arrives at the road overlooking the hospital from above. Several women are seen conversing outside the building. It is here that we finally see Satsuki and Mei's mother, a young woman in a plain kimono, with long hair, in the middle of writing a letter at the desk. She is the missing member with whom the family has been longing to reunite. The reason behind the family's excitement becomes obvious at this moment. The slight tinge of sadness that Hisaishi introduces in the melody and harmony of the image song, "Hey Let's Go," makes sense as well. As a child, Miyazaki (1988, 134) had felt anxious living with a mother suffering from severe illness. Many, including McCarthy (1999, 120) and Napier (2018, 9), have discussed how the director's own life experiences cast a long shadow in his works including *My Neighbor Totoro*. Perhaps Miyazaki repeatedly produced scenarios to cheer up young children as a recognition, based on his own experience, of the various unexpected challenges that they may have already encountered in their young lives. Could this predilection be considered a form of longing, a nostalgia for a happy childhood he never got to experience?

At the sight of her mother, Mei starts to run toward her and jumps into her lap. Satsuki approaches her mother more gingerly, her cheeks reddening slightly. Unlike her impulsive younger sister, Satsuki hesitates to express her excitement without being self-conscious. In these small details, Miyazaki depicts the different temperaments and levels of maturity of the two sisters. Their mother quickly reads Satsuki's feelings and thanks her for taking care of Mei's hair. She then takes a brush and offers to brush Satsuki's hair, remarking that her hair has a similar unruly texture (*kusekke*) as her own. Around this time, a new piece of music enters the aural space: a soft voice vocalizing a gentle melody on the syllable "ra" accompanied by a synthesizer [0:24:09]. This cue, included in the soundtrack album as "Mother" (S-8), is an arrangement of another song from the *Image Song Collection* with the same title, "Mother" (I-8), set to lyrics by Nakagawa.

Nakagawa's lyrics express Satsuki's strong desire to be reunited with her mother, touching on key moments from the film as well as from Satsuki's backstory. In the first stanza, for instance, the protagonist of the poem wishes to turn into a rabbit, so that she could leap into her mother's lap like Mei does in the film. The speaker also fantasizes about turning herself into a bird so she could fly across the blue sky to be close to her. In the film, the father's precarious navigation of the bicycle makes it seem as if Satsuki is, indeed, floating in air against the backdrop of a clear blue sky. The motif of animal transformation explored here returns later in the film when Satsuki writes a letter to her mother in which she imagines Mei turning into the impatient crab (Mei-gani) from the Japanese folktale "The Battle of Monkey and Crab." Nakagawa's text also alludes to things about Satsuki that are not revealed directly in the film. In the fourth stanza, the poem refers to the mother's magical fingers that can tame the speaker's hair into beautiful braids. The special emphasis on the neatness of the braids could be a reference to the mother's comment about Satsuki's unruly hair. In the backstory that Miyazaki had planned for the character, Satsuki used to have long braids. But once her mother was hospitalized, Satuski chopped off her hair so that she wouldn't have to worry about taking care of it and could spend more time taking care of various household chores (Kihara 2018, 50).

The straightforward, unadorned words and direct expression of admiration that Nakagawa uses in this poem is somewhat at odds with the way Satsuki speaks and behaves in the film. Mei who is the younger of the two feels free to indulge in her love and affection. On the other hand, Satsuki who strains to make herself useful for her family in this time of crisis, rarely expresses her desires and feelings directly. Even when she lets her mother comb her hair, she has to face away from her, occasionally turning her head to confirm her presence. The parents themselves notice Satsuki's emotional stress toward the end of the film. At least one Japanese commentator, too, remarks on this aspect of the family dynamics, worrying that Satsuki is reaching dangerously close to breaking point (Asano 2013, 21). Miyazaki too jokingly states that she would have turned into a teenage delinquent if she had not been rescued by Totoro (Miyazaki 1988, 137). Nakagawa's poem captures this tension that Satsuki feels between her strong urge to be reunited with her mother and her awareness of the need to restrain herself from expressing it openly. Satsuki's overwhelming emotions well up in a plain and simple statement of affection at the end of the poem, "I love you so much, my wonderful mother."

Hisaishi's setting of Nakagawa's lyrics closely mirrors the overall form of the poetry. Nakagawa's text alternates between stanzas relaying Satsuki's perception of her mother from a distance and stanzas describing the presence of the mother in close proximity. Hisaishi maintains this distinction by fashioning the song in a straightforward verse-chorus form that, for the most part, parallels the contrast between the distance from, and the closeness that Satsuki feels toward, her mother. Hisaishi also dramatizes the poem's intense yearning in the verse section employing many stylistic elements of Hisaishi melody, including his signature descending third sequence and chromatic chords. The melody rises higher and higher toward the end of the verse as Satsuki wishes to turn into a bird so she can fly toward her mother (0:42) (Example 8). The melody reaches its highest note up to that moment in the song, C above middle C, on the first syllable of the word "sky" (so-ra), reinforcing the notion of upward motion (0:45). As the voice glides down, Hisaishi introduces another chromatic chord in order to set the word "quickly" (hayaku), adding urgency to the end of the phrase (0:50). The rate of text setting relaxes by the final line of the verse creating a satisfactory rhythmic arc.

The song moves from verse to chorus without a break, shifting toward a happier mood that is inherent in Nakagawa's poem (0:58). In the verses, Nakagawa conveys Satsuki's wish to be reunited with her mother, who is understood to be in the distance. In the chorus, she presents the two in close proximity to one another. The melody in the chorus has a gently swaying syncopation, reminiscent of "My Neighbor Totoro." However, Satsuki's excitement comes through most clearly in the

Example 8 *"Mother" (I-8, 0:42), middle section of the first verse.*

increased rhythmic activities in the accompaniment part that features a rich array of instruments. The rhythmic pulsation of the percussion instrument adds to a sense of excitement and optimism, as opposed to nervousness, to the chorus. The source of the metallic twinkling sound is less obvious, but nevertheless, it adds to the textual density of the passage that reflects Satsuki's heightened emotional state.

Harmonically, Hisaishi does away with the melancholic descending third sequence in the chorus section. Instead, the bass line leaps downward at the outset from E♭ to G and from there, moves stepwise to B♭. However, he continues to use a modal mixture chord (A♭m6) in the middle of the phrase (1:05). The vocal melody of the chorus ends by landing on E♭, the tonic note of the key, but the harmony supporting it is an unexpected A♭ chord approached from a G chord, suggesting a deceptive motion (1:22). The gesture delays the harmonic resolution of the piece for a few more measures. These harmonic quirks, characteristic of Hisaishi melody, cast a shadow on Satsuki's happy thoughts, evoking her bittersweet sentiment. Hisaishi sets Nakagawa's fifth and final stanza, which provides another picture of the mother from a distance, as another statement of the chorus, departing from the pattern that he had established earlier (2:50). This break from the established pattern, however, adds a sense of urgency. The song ends somewhat optimistically, with a substantial coda in which the synthesizer, with its buzzy sound and rich vibrato, plays the first half of the verse melody (3:19).

In the film, the cue derived from the image song continues through a sequence showing the family's return trip along a road surrounded by beautiful green tea plants [0:24:36]. Inoue's gentle vocalization of the melody blends with the laughter of Satsuki, Mei, and their father. Even though the mother is not with them, the music reminds us of her warm presence.

"A Lost Child" (I-4)

Later in the summer, Satsuki and Mei receive the unexpected news that their mother's planned visit must be canceled because of her worsening condition. The two sisters express their disappointment in different ways. Satsuki becomes anxious and despondent, while Mei turns petulant and combative, peppering her big sister with questions she cannot answer. Unable to hide her disappointment and frustration any longer, Satsuki yells at Mei, asking if she wanted her mother dead, and runs away. Left behind with Kanta, Mei launches into a crying fit and starts to walk back to her house. Later, Mei witnesses Satsuki crying on Granny's shoulder. This is a shocking sight for Mei. Not only her mother but also her usually reliable big sister are in danger. Mei decides to leave the house to deliver the corn she had picked earlier that day to her mother. Granny had told her that her mother would certainly feel better if she ate the corn. This starts the climactic episode of *My Neighbor Totoro*, Satsuki's desperate search for Mei.

Hisaishi inserts two brief cues to portray Satsuki's fear and anxiety, based on the image song, "A Lost Child" (Maigo, I-4), with lyrics by Nakagawa, included on the *Image Song Collection*. The direct source for the two cues is the instrumental track, "A Lost Child," arranged for conventional orchestral instruments and the recorder by Hirabe. This track is included in the *Soundtrack Album* with the title "Mei Is Missing" (Mei ga inai, S-16) along with Inoue's sung version of the song (S-12), although the latter does not appear in the film.

While the title, "A Lost Child," might suggest that the song is about Mei, the child who gets lost in the film, Nakagawa's poem actually conveys Satsuki's feelings of helplessness when she suddenly realizes that her younger sister is nowhere to be seen. Throughout the poem, Nakagawa uses the Japanese word *imōto* (younger sister) to refer to the lost child, suggesting that the poem is written from Satsuki's viewpoint. The first and third stanzas describe Satsuki's awareness of Mei's disappearance in the present moment. The alternating second and fourth stanzas as well as the final fifth stanza dwells, instead, on Satsuki's memories of her younger sister. These stanzas also express Satsuki's heartfelt desire to be reunited with Mei, ending with the question "where can she be?" The similarity to "Mother" can be observed not only in the urgency of Satsuki desire but also in the way she toggles back and forth between expressing her feelings in the present moment and indulging in fond recollections of the past.

Hisaishi conveys Satsuki's sense of being at a loss through his careful musical treatment of Nakagawa's text. As in his setting of "Mother," Hisaishi fashions a song based on the verse-chorus form that reflects the temporal juxtapositions in Nakagawa's poem. The song starts with a single melody played on the harp that rises up and falls down, undulating in a seemingly meandering and purposeless manner. The sound of the plucked strings of the harp echoes in such a way as to convey a sense of loneliness at the outset of the piece. Hisaishi chooses the minor key of F to convey the mournful tone of Nakagawa's poem. The verse begins with his favorite chord progression, the descending third sequence, but it breaks off after three chords, shifting the tonality temporarily to A♭ major (0:23; Example 9). This harmonic design introduces a tonal ambiguity, an unpredictable bass motion, as well as frequent chord changes, adding to Satsuki's mounting sense of anxiety. This unsettled harmonic trajectory of the verse parallels Satsuki's frantic search for her sister, taking her to different parts of the countryside. Satsuki's unease is reflected in her being unable to remain rested in a single key.

On the other hand, a contrasting mood in the chorus section speaks to Satsuki's sense of hopefulness (0:52). As in "Mother," Hisaishi increases the number of instruments accompanying Inoue's voice in the chorus. The subdued instrumentation of the verse section consists of harp, electric bass, and synthesizer strings. In the chorus, the composer adds the sounds of a resonant bass drum and marimba riffs that give this piece an unexpected "minimal and ethnic" touch. The harmonic structure of the chorus is much more evenly measured and relaxed. Rather than his usual descending third sequence, Hisaishi harmonizes the bass line using mostly major triads that endow the chorus with a brighter, more optimistic tinge (Example 10). Hisaishi concludes the chorus

Example 9 *"A Lost Child" (I-4, 0:14), the opening measures of the first verse.*

Ka-ku - ren - bo ga da - i - su - ki

Example 10 *"A Lost Child" (I-4, 0:52), the opening measures of the first chorus.*

with the setting of Nakagawa's line, "Where could she be?" to a hesitantly rising melodic fragment resting on an A♭ (1:16). The first two iterations of the chorus conclude the phrase in A♭ major. The third and last presentation of the chorus, however, reinterprets the note as part of an F minor chord (3:09). The coda, which consists of the melody from the verse on a reedy instrument, continues the piece in F minor but concludes on an F major chord giving us a sense of hopefulness at the end.

In the film, Mei's disappearance is signaled by the increasingly concerned voices of Satsuki and Granny, looking for Mei, piercing through the incessant cries of the cicadas. Satsuki eventually leaves her home in search of Mei and climbs up a small hill in order to have a higher view. The sound of the cicadas continues while the camera pans to show the gorgeous vista of the bucolic landscape, bathed in the brilliant lights of the setting sun. Mixed into this is a faint echo of the temple bell in the distance. The first musical cue begins here, almost imperceptibly. It is an instrumental arrangement of "A Lost Child," featuring the timbres of the harp, recorder, and oboe. Even though the text of the song is suppressed, the mournful timbre of the oboe, combined with the crimson skies of a summer twilight, convey the sense of loss. This instrumental cue, however, is short-lived. The oboe plays the first half of the verse, and the strings take over the second half, while the camera follows Satsuki running through the narrow winding roads, passing various landmarks from earlier in the film. The cue reaches its premature end, however, when Satsuki bumps into a young couple driving from the direction of the hospital. This abrupt end is a signal for the audience to pay attention.

At this point, Kanta enters the scene riding a bicycle. The news that he bears is even more upsetting: Granny found what may be Mei's sandal in a nearby pond. The camera shows an image of a small pink sandal floating in the pond, another rare moment of diegetic presentation of an image, followed by a close-up of Satsuki. This unusual visual gesture underscores Satsuki's anguish. Music reenters at this precise moment with the harp introduction over a string tremolo adding to the tension of the scene. When Satsuki begins to run, the oboe and then the strings play the melody of the verse. The cue here is almost identical to the second half of the orchestral arrangement of "A Lost Child" made by Hirabe, included on the *Soundtrack Album*. The transition from verse to chorus coincides with the cut to Granny praying on her knees while holding the sandal tightly in her hands. Hisaishi, however, truncates the chorus, ending the cue when Satsuki reaches the villagers gathered at the pond and calls out to Granny. The track included on the *Soundtrack Album*, however, contains the arrangement of the entire chorus section.

Throughout this episode, Hisaishi's music does not have any significant sync points that match the action depicted in the film. For instance, the tempo of the music is much slower than the rate at which Satsuki runs. It remains steady and does not fluctuate when Satsuki slows down or speeds up. In composing his cue for Mei's chase for the Totoro earlier in the film, Hisaishi followed every move and gesture of the young child in order to create a humorous effect. In this episode, however, the contrast between the lyrically expansive melody of the song and the urgency expressed in Satsuki's running enhances the poignancy of each. At the same time, Hisaishi's coordination of the chorus, the emotional high point of the song, with Granny's prayer suggests his desire to match the affective intensity of both the music and the narrative.

* * *

Like many other elements of this film, Miyazaki drew inspiration for this episode from his own experience. Miyazaki (1988, 138) recalls a memory from his childhood when his younger brother got lost when the family went to a *bon* festival. The family members split up and searched for the child. As night fell, the search became particularly difficult. Eventually, the brother was found safe but upset, clinging on to an older woman who herself did not know what to do. Although the episode had a happy ending as in the film, it appears to have left a deep impression on the young Miyazaki. Experiences like this one and those described in the film—temporarily getting lost or losing someone close to you—are common to many people. Despite their ordinariness, such events can register extreme emotional anxiety, especially when experienced as a child or involving loved ones. This scene gains its power to elicit strong emotions not only because it deals with the commonest of life's anxieties but also because Hisaishi's music lends it his particular patina of nostalgia.

6 Forgotten Sounds

In addition to the six compositions discussed in the previous chapters, the *Image Song Collection* includes three more songs that allude to various genres of American popular music. These are "The Catbus" (Nekobasu, I-6) in the style of early rock and roll, "Dondoko Festival" (Dondoko Matsuri, I-10) in the style of the blues, and "Fushigi Shiritori Song" (Fushigi shiritori uta, I-7) in the style of funk. Such stylistic diversity is not surprising, considering that Japanese listeners and musicians have been voraciously consuming and adapting various styles of American popular music for well over a century. On this film soundtrack, however, many of these stylistic references disappeared as a result of changes in arrangements, editing, or elimination of entire songs. Nevertheless, Hisaishi added another cue, "The Village in May" (Gogatsu no mura, S-2) also included on the soundtrack album, which is evocative of jazz. These songs and cues provide yet another layer of meaning and nostalgia to the film.

"The Catbus" (I-6)

Dating from 1975, the Catbus was one of the earliest illustrations that Miyazaki made for *My Neighbor Totoro*

(Miyazaki 2018, 3). At this early planning stage, Miyazaki had not yet fully developed the image of Totoro. On the other hand, Miyazaki's idea for the Catbus was already fully fleshed out, but its shape was different from the figure we see in the film. This early Catbus, the 1975 model, has many more limbs that are much shorter and stubbier compared to its final form. The pair of ears are placed above a single large rectangular opening that resembles a windshield as opposed to being positioned right above the eyes. This early Catbus also has a fox-like driver with a pointed snout and other monstrous customers, anticipating the steamboat that carries a myriad of Japanese deities in *Spirited Away*. It carries a bumper with a number plate bearing the image of a *torii* gate. There are also familiar elements in this version of the Catbus. Its eyes function as headlights, it has two rats at the top providing additional lighting, and perhaps most importantly, it wears a wide grin that stretches across its entire face.

Even though Miyazaki conceives the Catbus as a supernatural creature tied to the landscape of Japan, it represents a unique blend of the familiar and the unfamiliar, straddling categories of both the native and the foreign. Take its Japanese name *Nekobasu*, for instance. It is a bilingual portmanteau that combines a Japanese word for cat (*neko*) and the word bus (*basu*) borrowed from English. It is a chimeric figure that draws on ancient Japanese folklore about cats' magical ability to shapeshift but also alludes to the imported modern technology of the motor bus. It is an uncanny blend of a living animal and an inanimate object. As a manifestation of the wind, the Catbus is visible to Satsuki and Mei but invisible to the others. It has the ability to push objects around, but, like the wind, it is also immaterial and can evaporate into thin air. In sum, the Catbus is a liminal, in-between character that exists in multiple categories that are often understood to be oppositional.[1]

In the film, Miyazaki continues to highlight the Catbus's ambiguous state of being in its sound design. On the one hand, Miyazaki associates the Catbus with the naturalistic sounds including cat-like growls and the sounds of strong gusts of wind. On the other hand, the Catbus is accompanied by a musical cue (derived from Hisaishi and Nakagawa's song "The Catbus") in the style of early rock'n'roll, highlighting the foreignness of the creature against its domestic natural habitat. Yet in the 1950s, when the film is set, Japan witnessed a surge in popularity for rockabilly. Hisaishi's allusion to this style of music, which was old-fashioned by the late 1980s, has the potential to arouse a nostalgic reaction from older viewers. However, Hirabe's arrangement of the song in the film substitutes Hisaishi's rock'n'roll instrumentation for a symphonic jazz piece.

Nakagawa's poem for the image song "The Catbus" emphasizes the duality of the Catbus as a living creature and a machine. Nakagawa lists various physical features of the Catbus as well as its incredible abilities, making her poem sound like a song for a car commercial. The Catbus's impressive "specs" include bright yellow headlights, a fancy coat, and shiny whiskers. Its incredible speed, agility, and maneuverability allow it to dash through the dark, fly through the sky, jump over a shooting star, and even perform midair summersaults. Zooming from one corner of the world to another at a supernatural speed, the Catbus also offers spectacular views for its passengers. Yet Nakagawa is quick to point out the Catbus's large grin as well as the cat-like growl (*nyāgo*), reminding us that the Catbus is a living creature. Nakagawa's poem also implies that the Catbus is in control of its movement rather than being controlled by a driver. This suggestion of agency makes the Catbus less machine-like.

Of all the poems that Nakagawa composed for the image album, the Catbus song has the most borrowed words derived from English. These include the words "bus" (*basu*), "headlights" (*heddoraito*), "handle" (*handoru*), and "curve" (*kābu*). In written Japanese, borrowed words like these are presented in a distinct syllabary called *katakana* that visually stands out from the rest of the text. These words, therefore, not only sound but also *look* different, giving the poem an obvious sense of foreignness associated with modernity and stylishness. Nakagawa emphasizes the fanciness and novelty of this new mode of transportation when she adds that even the otherwise "merry monsters (*obake*)" put on slight airs when they are on the bus. The image of indigenous Japanese monsters acting in this manner not only provides humor to the song but also points to the interesting tension between the categories of native and foreign that the Catbus embodies.

The music Hisaishi provided for this image song is unlike any piece discussed so far, avoiding overt references to his signature styles of "minimal and ethnic" or Hisaishi melody. The sign that we are far from Hisaishi's signature lyric style is in the song's simple harmonic palette, which basically consists of four chords: A, D, E7, and its variant E/A. The form of the song is simple, consisting of an introduction, two sets of verse and chorus, the reprise of the first chorus, and a coda. The verses are in the thirty-two-bar song form (AABA) frequently seen in American popular songs, making use of a predictable harmonic progression typical of 1950s rock-n-roll songs (Example 11). The chorus is much briefer, consisting of only eight measures, but presenting all four chords in rapid succession. The variety of chords and the rate at which they change in this song are much slower compared to other songs in the collection such as "My Neighbor Totoro" or "The Path of the Wind."

Like the simple melodic form and harmonic pattern of the song, the song's timbral combination seems out of sync with Hisaishi's customary style, at least at the outset. The brief introduction is made up of a syncopated electric guitar riff that oscillates between D♯ and E (Example 12). Hisaishi deploys two types of guitar sounds here: one that sounds plucked and deadened, and another with a distorted, twangy reverb. Combined with the emphatic drum beat at the top of the measure, the guitar riff points to the sounds of American rock bands such as the Beach Boys and the Ventures. The Ventures, in particular, created an "electric guitar boom" in Japan in the 1960s (Stevens 2008, 43). In Hisaishi's song, the sound world

Example 11 *"The Catbus" (I-6, 0:15), the opening measures of the first verse.*

Example 12 *"The Catbus" (I-6), the opening guitar riff.*

of the Ventures-inspired instrumental rock lasts only for a brief moment, quickly replaced by an array of synthesized sounds. As in other pieces by him, Hisaishi gradually adds new sounds to thicken the texture as the song progresses. Notable among them is the addition of the piano-like sound in the bridge of the verse that continues into the chorus section. Hisaishi also adds video-game-like sound effects in the track. These include the percussive "bloopy" sound and the metallic sound that emits a rapid circular chromatic twirling, adding not only to the humor but also to the otherworldliness of the piece. The guitar riffs from the intro return at the song's conclusion, bringing back the song's association with surf music.

The Catbus appears twice in the film. In both cases, the Catbus emerges after Large Totoro's primal screams, but the manner in which it is represented in music and sound is distinct each time. The first time around, Totoro howls in delight after hearing the torrential sound of water falling on the umbrella [0:53:13]. Here, the entrance of the Catbus is not marked by a musical cue but by the loud sounds of the blowing wind. The sound of the wind continues for a short while after the creature has stopped in front of the bus stop. This makes sense since the Catbus registers as a sudden gust of wind to those who cannot see it. The scene originally had a cue Hisaishi composed based on the image song. However, the music had an unintended result of turning the Catbus into a "happy and silly cat, a foreign cat" (Miyazaki 1988, 130) that destroyed the mood of mystery. In the end, the creative team decided to suppress the song, enhancing Satsuki and Mei's wonderment mixed with fear when coming face to face with the Catbus.

The second time the Catbus appears is when Totoro screams at the top of the camphor tree responding to Satsuki's plea to help her find her younger sister. The Catbus's entrance is marked by the only cue based on Hisaishi's image song "The Catbus" in the film [1:19:00]. Hirabe's arrangement of the image song for full orchestra eradicates the song's former association with the sounds of surf music. This symphonic arrangement of the song is also included on the soundtrack album with the same title "The Catbus" (S-17). McCarthy (1999, 135) calls this a "boogie-woogie any jazzman could pick up on and relish." Muted trumpets present the melody over the active and vivacious accompaniment figure, whose repetitive rhythm gives off an impression of a locomotive in motion. The violins indulge in upward melodic swoops in the bridge section, reflecting the Catbus's swagger and confidence that contrasts with the emotional distress of Satsuki.

Once Satsuki boards the Catbus, the music switches to a solo piano rendition of the song. It is as if we are listening to muzak playing in the background of the bus [1:19:40]. The syncopated melody of "The Catbus" makes the solo piano sound like a ragtime, giving an old-timey feel to Satsuki's journey. The music eventually dies down as Satsuki's initial shock and excitement subsides, giving way to the sounds of the wind. She turns her eyes outside of the bus and sees that the destination sign at the front of the bus has switched to "Mei." The orchestral arrangement of the song resumes immediately at this point as well to indicate Satsuki's joy at realizing what Totoro and the Catbus are promising to do [1:20:08]. The jolly music continues until the Catbus delivers Satsuki to Mei.

"Fushigi Shiritori Song" (I-7)

The word "fushigi" from the title of "Fushigi Shiritori Song" is a Buddhist term used to describe something that is beyond ordinary human comprehension. It has multiple connotations of strangeness, mystery, and wonderment (Figal 1999, 223–24n6); for example, it appears in the translation of the title for Lewis Carroll's *Alice in Wonderland* (*Fushigi no kuni no Arisu*). The word "shiritori" alludes to a Japanese word game which literally means "bottom snatching." The players are required to say a word that starts with the *kana* script (either hiragana or katakana) that ends the previous word, its metaphorical "bottom." The game continues until a player inadvertently says a word that ends with the *kana* "n." For instance, if the first player starts the game with the word "Nekobasu," the next player has to say another word that starts with the *kana* "su" such as "Susuwatari." The following player is then required to say another word by taking the "bottom" of the previous word, in this case "ri," and putting it at the front of another.

Despite its title, however, Nakagawa's poem does not follow the rules of *shiritori*. It starts with an ambiguous, seemingly paradoxical statement, acknowledging that there are so many strange and mysterious things that it's no longer strange. This statement stands alone as a short stanza. In the following stanza, the poem launches into a circular series of word associations: many strange things (*fushigi ga takusan*) are creepy (*bukimi*), creepy things are scary (*kowai*), scary things are monsters (*obake*), monsters are ghosts (*yūrei*), and ghosts are creepy. It is as if the protagonist of the poem has distorted the rules that govern the game of *shiritori* to create an alternative word game. The circular development of these word associations suggests that the song can, theoretically, go on forever. Nakagawa abruptly ends the game and describes the visceral and emotional reactions of the protagonist, presumably Satsuki and Mei. Suddenly the girls perceive someone next to them. Whether it is a ghost or a monster, they declare, they are not afraid of it. The courageous declaration at the end of the stanza brings to mind Satsuki and Mei's screaming in the attic of the house they have just moved into.

The following stanza repeats the pattern of the second but starts with the word "creepy" (*bukimi*) instead of "strange" (*fushigi*) and continues the modified version of *shiritori*: creepy things are strange, strange things are fun (*yukai*), fun is interesting (*omoshiroi*), interesting things are ghosts, and ghosts are strange. This round of word association repeats some key ideas from the previous game, but also signals the shift in the girls' perception of the "ghosts" as being fun and interesting, attesting to the fearless nature of the sisters. The stanza concludes with the description of a mysterious figure with large hands and long nails behind them. Again, the line brings to mind the scene from the film when Satsuki senses the presence of Large Totoro and sees its hand and nails from beneath her umbrella. The regular structure of the poem falls apart after this point.

While Hisaishi casts many of the songs in the collection in a simple verse-chorus form, the musical structure of "Fushigi Shiritori Song" is harder to analyze. The complexity is partly due to the irregular shape of Nakagawa's poem. The song starts with Hisaishi's signature minimalist marimba riff followed by a chant-like, monotonous vocal melody (Example 13).

Fu - shi - gi   fu - shi - gi   fu - shi - gi   da - ra - ke   de   fu - shi - gi   ja   nai

Example 13 *"Fushigi Shiritori Song" (I-7, 0:04), the opening measures of the first stanza.*

The musical setting of the second stanza itself has multiple discrete segments of various lengths:

1) the repetition of the introductory refrain but set to a slightly different text (0:22);

2) the string of associated words (the *shiritori* proper, 0:31);

3) a brief instrumental interlude (0:40);

4) the girls' reactions (0:43);

5) an extended percussion solo (0:52); and

6) the final four lines of the stanza, in which the girls declare their fearlessness (1:00).

Despite these irregularities, Hisaishi organizes the music in a regular four-measure pattern. Yet, the insertion of the brief instrumental interlude (segment 3) that lasts only for a single measure, disturbs this evenly phrased pattern, contributing yet another element of strangeness to the mix. The remainder of the song mirrors the complicated formal structure of Nakagawa's poem.

Another source of confusion is Hisaishi's use of an unexpectedly wide array of vocal and instrumental timbres. This contributes to a unique style that makes this song stand out from the rest of the pieces on the album. As in other numbers, Hisaishi adds different instrumental parts, layer by layer, as the piece progresses. The gradual unfolding of the instrumental combination keeps the listener guessing the stylistic references of this piece. Shortly following the minimalist marimba riffs discussed above, Hisaishi introduces a hi-hat and then synth drums, providing a powerful rhythmic drive characteristic of 1980s rock. The electric bass guitar enters the accompaniment texture at the top of the second stanza, slapping and popping in a funky style. Also alluding to funk are the heavily accented synthesized horn licks that enter in a call-and-response at the end of the word association game. The extended four-measure interlude within the second stanza (segment 5) is an oddly empty-sounding drum solo. The singer on this album, Mori Kumiko, uses her powerful and robust voice to belt and shout, deforming vowel sounds at ends of phrases. A backup chorus of male voices doubles Mori throughout the track. Another odd feature is the sound of a child's voice, which suddenly emerges at the top of the fourth stanza (3:00) and traverses through space from right to left. These unexpected gestures create an eerie sonic landscape for the composition, adding to Hisaishi's creative synthesis of seemingly disparate elements.

One concrete model that Hisaishi may have taken into consideration is a particular arrangement of the theme song from the popular animation series *Gegege no kitarō* by Mizuki Shigeru, an influential manga artist recognized as "Japan's foremost creator of ghost stories" (Schodt 2012, 15). The theme song for the TV series, composed by Izumi Taku based on the lyrics by Mizuki, exists in multiple versions according to different series. The third series, which aired from 1985 to 1988, used an arrangement of the song by Nomura Yutaka sung by the *enka* singer Yoshi Ikuzō, then known mostly for his comic novelty song, "I'm Going to Tokyo" (Ora Tokyo sa iguda). The series was produced by Tōei Animation and the single of the song was released in 1985 by Tokuma Japan Communications.[2] This version, contemporaneous with *My Neighbor Totoro*, features strong drumbeats, a prominent electric bass line, and pungent synthesized horn riffs, all elements of "Fushigi Shiritori Song."

Mizuki's *Gegege no Kitarō* is a humorous but often disturbing treatment of traditional Japanese monsters and ghosts called *yōkai*. Mizuki's work, which first appeared in print as manga and soon after as TV anime in the late 1960s, became an enormous hit in Japan (Papp 2010, 105). The thematic connection between Mizuki's anime and "Fushigi Shiritori Song" is obvious. Indeed, some of Miyazaki's early sketches include images of *yōkai*-like Japanese monsters aboard the Catbus. However, Miyazaki (1988, 125) was quick to point out that he tried to avoid making Totoro into a grotesque *yōkai* in the manner of Mizuki. Even Granny reassures the Kusakabe family that the *susuwatari* are *not* something scary like a *yōkai*. Perhaps because of Miyazaki's opposition to the idea of the *yōkai*, the song was dropped entirely from the soundtrack of the film despite its fascinating musical characteristics.

"Dondoko Festival" (I-10)

Of all the songs in the *Image Song Collection*, "Dondoko Festival" is perhaps the most perplexing one. The song lyrics are attributed to neither Nakagawa nor Miyazaki but to the "W. City

Production Department" (W. Shitī Sēsakubu). The song lyrics depict one of the iconic scenes from the film: the mysterious nighttime ritual of the trio of Totoro casting a magic spell on the acorns in the ground, as told from the girls' perspective. The narrator of the song calls the ritual "*dondoko* matsuri," combining an onomatopoeic word "dondoko" (describing the sounds of a *taiko* drum) and the word *matsuri* ("festival," traditionally having strong religious connotations in Shinto practice; Robertson 1991, 39). The title can thus point to the festive nature of the ritual but also suggests that it is supernatural. The song continues, describing the protagonists jumping into the yard to join the monsters. As in the film, the acorns that were planted in the ground begin to sprout and grow. The final stanza of the song invites the listeners to join in onm the dance, reassuring them that they too will one day meet monsters like these. Such an invitation to the audience is consonant with the sentiment expressed in "My Neighbor Totoro."

Musically, the song is a fascinating hybrid of Japanese traditional taiko drumming—an instrument loaded with connotations of Japanese folk music (Bender 2012)—and the American blues. The reference to taiko drumming comes in the instrumental introduction in duple meter (Example 14). The drumbeats are interspersed with distorted samples of male voices, inserted on the second and fourth beat in a manner reminiscent of *kakegoe* (also heard in "Susuwatari"). The obviously synthetic sound of the *kakegoe,* however, gives the introduction a strange, eerie feel, suggesting that this is no ordinary festival. It also ties the song to "Susuwatari," in which Hisaishi claims to have used the sampled voices of the "pygmy" people.

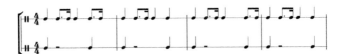

Example 14 *"Dondoko Festival" (I-10), percussion rhythm.*

Example 15 *"Dondoko Festival" (I-10, 0:39), the opening measures of the sung melody.*

The instrumental introduction then moves to the presentation of the sung melody accompanied by an intricate call-and-response texture on a solo harmonica and an electric lead guitar (0:39; Example 15). The harmonic palette of the introduction is limited to three chords: E, A7, and B. The harmonic pattern does not follow the traditional form of the twelve-bar blues, but it contains a stylistically characteristic dominant-to-subdominant shift, in this case B to A7, before the final cadence. The form of this piece becomes even more challenging to determine once the vocalist, Inoue, enters. The harmonic palette remains limited, except for the addition of the G#m and F#m7 chords that give the piece harmonic variety. This four-minute-long piece also has an extensive coda, featuring solos by the guitar and the harmonica, although the musicians are not credited on the album (3:09).

The song makes an appearance in the film in an extremely pared down form during the ritual under the moonlit sky. The faint sounds of the drum are heard before Satsuki realizes that something is happening in the yard [0:57:16]. The music is the isolated track of the drumming from "Dondoko Festival."

The role of the music here is puzzling. The trio of Totoro are not seen playing any drums, and their rhythmic bobbing and jumping do not correspond to the drumbeats. Soon after, as the camera cuts from Satsuki's vantage point from her room looking into the yard to the image of the Totoro in the yard, the ambient music from "Totoro's Theme" enters the soundscape [0:57:35]. Hisaishi does not align the two tracks of music metrically in any way. The drumming pattern is in 4/4 time while "Totoro's Theme" is in 7/4 time. It would have been possible to align the beats of the two parts but here the two are simply layered on one another creating a far more complex rhythmic expression. Again, the temporal organization of the music does not coincide in any obvious manner with the actions on the screen, creating a loose, asynchronous relationship between the image and the sound. The music is familiar because of the drumming, inviting the girls to join in the dance. The music is unfamiliar because of the combination of synthesized sustained notes, organ sounds, voice, and marimba (See Chapter 3). Finally, the asynchrony of the music and the image creates a disorienting, dream-like atmosphere.

There is one instance, however, where a significant synchrony takes place between the image and the music. At one point, Totoro and the girls lift their arms up to coax the acorns in the ground to sprout. The sprouts come up with popping sound effects, but they are not synchronized to the music in the background. The camera cuts to Large Totoro exerting all of its might, holding the black umbrella and lifting it up. His hair stands up and he shivers all over. When the camera cuts to the ground, a group of sprouts comes in rapid succession. The popping of the first sprout is timed exactly to a statement of synthesized "ah" from Totoro's theme [0:58:23]. Because of the rarity of such calculated temporal coordination between music and image, the synchrony here points to the significance of the moment when the girls witness the life-giving power of Totoro's magic.

The mysterious music for the Dondoko Festival continues for a bit longer as the trio of Totoro and the girls encourage the sprouts to grow into saplings, and the saplings into trees. The cue, however, cross-cuts with an orchestrated version of "The Path of the Wind," overlapping briefly for about four seconds. The second cue is mixed at a much higher level. The more conventional orchestration also helps draw in the audience into emotional alignment with the scene, while the music for the Dondoko Festival recedes into the background. In this cue, the vocals and any sign of the song's sonic affinities to the American blues are suppressed entirely.

"The Village in May" (S-2)

The first piece of music we hear in the film after the opening theme song is an orchestral cue called "The Village in May" (S-2), composed by Hisaishi and arranged by Hirabe. The cue does not derive from the songs in the *Image Song Collection* and seems to have been newly composed for the soundtrack of the film; it only exists in instrumental form. This lengthy cue follows the progress of the Kusakabe family's move through the countryside. Miyazaki delights in showing the viewers the beauty of nature in a Japanese farming village, following the antiquated motorized tricycle bus through the winding roads, passing rice paddies, and swinging around an old *inari* shrine

The environment depicted in the film points to a specific time and place: the Japanese countryside in the late 1950s. However, the music that accompanies this sequence is at odds with this characterization [0:02:56]. The music is in the style of a pleasant but somewhat anodyne jazz piece, reminiscent of soundtracks from countless TV programs. The piece is in a simple ABA form with a brief intro. The introduction features high woodwind instruments (flute and oboe) playing a lilting syncopated melody doubled on the bell-like sounds of the glockenspiel. In the A section the violins play a delightful rising main melody, engaging in a call-and-response with the woodwinds playing a contrasting descending riff (0:15; Example 16). The brass instruments punctuate the texture, occasionally with bluesy chromatic gestures. The B section employs a series of sweeping upward gestures as if we are witnessing a dance (1:00). The music itself is wonderful but seems to contradict the traditionally "Japanese" image presented on the screen, adding to the notion about the effort of Hisaishi to present a culturally unspecific (or unidentifiable) soundtrack. The music returns later in the film to accompany the girls in action while they finish cleaning the house on the move-in day [0:15:56].

The Japanese title of the cue, "Gogatsu no Mura," however, can be seen as a pun on the word "May" which is related to the names of the sisters, Satsuki and Mei. "Satsuki" is the traditional name for the fifth month of the year in the Japanese calendar. "Mei" is a Japanese transliteration of the English word "May." The title of the cue uses the less poetic but more common name

Example 16 *"The Village in May" (S-2, 0:15), the opening measures of the A section.*

for May, *gogatsu* (literally, the fifth month). In other words, the title could be read as "Satsuki's Village" or "Mei's Village." Yet the music, with an American sound, seems oddly out of step with the depiction of the Japanese countryside from the past. In fact, early reviewers of the soundtrack album in the *Animage* magazine complained that the cue sounds oddly Disney-esque (Suishō and Yamamoto 1988, 190). One way to reconcile this curious mismatch is to understand it as the musical representation of Satsuki and Mei's sense of displacement from their older home. In other words, the two sisters, moving from the big city to the countryside, might as well be foreigners in an unfamiliar land. In fact, the entire family stands out like a sore thumb. Not only is the mother absent, but the father is depicted as an easygoing and somewhat unworldly figure with an unconventional, irregular work schedule as a scholar and a university professor.

Nevertheless, the use of a jazz-inspired cue at this moment certainly points to the long and at times complicated history of jazz in Japan (Atkins 2001). Loved and popularized during the Taishō and early Shōwa eras (1920s and 1930s), jazz was suppressed in Japan during the Pacific War due to its association with the United States. Immediately following the war, starting during the long period of American occupation, the popularity of jazz experienced a resurgence especially with the new influx of American soldier musicians and touring artists. By the time the film was set, in the late 1950s, jazz was once again one of the major genres of popular music in Japan. However, the style of jazz presented in this cue points to the prewar era rather than bebop or other cutting-edge style of jazz that would have been present in the country at that time. This fact alone points to the complicated history of "Westernization" of Japanese musical taste. But for the film specifically, the antiquity of the music definitely adds to the sense of temporal distance between the world that the audience inhabits and the world depicted in the film. It also exaggerates this temporal distance. In this manner, it perhaps contributes to creating a nostalgic hue in the soundscape of the film.

* * *

Being familiar with the film before the image album, listening to the songs "The Catbus," "Fushigi Shiritori Song," and "Dondoko Festival" turned out to be a pleasant surprise for me. It was as if I had stumbled upon a completely foreign world hidden in plain sight. These songs demonstrate Hisaishi's chameleon-like ability to absorb and master musical styles of various genres of American popular music that the Japanese public have been consuming and producing avidly for more than a century and a half. Paying attention to the alterations that were made to "The Catbus" and "Dondoko Festival" as well as the outright elimination of "Fushigi Shiritori Song" from the soundtrack of *My Neighbor Totoro* makes us aware of the lengthy and complicated process Hisaishi undertook in order to create music for the film. While the image album, containing songs in the style of early rock 'n' roll, the blues, and even funk, demonstrates Hisaishi's eclectic musical taste, his soundtrack for the film focuses more narrowly on his signature Hisaishi melody and "minimal and ethnic" style, with an occasional nod to light jazz. This transformation demonstrates one of the major goals of producing an image album that Takahata saw—an opportunity for the composer and the director to try out different musical ideas and how they fit the concept of the film (see Chapter 1). The paring down of stylistic references helped to give the music for *My Neighbor Totoro* a more unified sound and, in the end, a more distinct sonic signature to the film. Nevertheless, despite the title of this chapter, the songs that were altered or eliminated are never really forgotten. In fact, the continued availability of the *Image Song Collection* ensures that we can still enjoy these songs in their original forms.

Conclusion: Forgetting and Remembering

On April 16, 1988, *My Neighbor Totoro* opened in theaters in Japan as a double feature with Takahata Isao's *Grave of the Fireflies*. The latter was based on a 1967 semiautobiographical novella by Nosaka Akiyuki, about the struggle of two orphaned siblings, Seita and Setsuko, to survive during the final days of the Second World War and their deaths shortly after its conclusion. The beautifully rendered yet achingly poignant tone of the film creates a stark contrast with the buoyant mood of *Totoro*. The two production teams within Studio Ghibli worked side by side to complete the films, which were promoted with the unifying tagline "We've come to deliver something forgotten."

Archives of Studio Ghibli (1996, 78–81) includes several drafts of the tagline. These explore different sets of concerns about marketing two films that differ greatly from each other in style and content. One prominent theme was the preoccupation with appealing to multiple generations of audience members. Several of them addressed the parents, oddly fathers only, encouraging them to watch the films with their children: "To Baby Boomer dads (*dankon no sedai no oyaji tachi yo*), we want you to see these two films with children" and "To Baby Boomer dads, your kids will seek 'you' in history." Some of them addressed both the fathers and their children: "We want to show you! To your children, to your dads." Others dealt with the thorny issue of history and memory. One startling example boldly states: "The word nostalgia (*nosutaruji*) did not exist in this era."

In the end, the creative team settled on the unified tagline that captures the nostalgic impulses in both films. However, viewers experience different kinds of emotional resonance when watching these two films and perceiving that "something forgotten." One particularly poignant musical cue in *Grave of the Fireflies* comes toward the end of the film when Amelia Galli-Curci's prewar recording of Henry Bishop's song, "Home! Sweet Home!" is heard. In this scene, three well-to-do young sisters return to their house and joyously put a record on the phonograph while repeating the key word, "*natsukashii*" ("doesn't this bring back memories?"). The music takes over the soundtrack as the camera pans out to show the deserted "home" of the two siblings, a primitive evacuation shelter dug into the banks of a lake. Suddenly, a vision of the dead sister, Setsuko, emerges, engaging in a series of childlike activities. The serene voice of Galli-Curci singing a song about homesickness creates a powerful contrast against the haunting vision of Setsuko. The juxtaposition reminds us that what has happened cannot be undone. The film seems to suggest that the past is irrevocable, and that nostalgia cannot bring back a dead child.

In her monograph, *The Future of Nostalgia*, cultural historian Svetlana Boym (2001, 337) explores the concept which she calls the "poethics of nostalgia." Boym argues that nostalgia can cultivate a person's ability to empathize with another through a shared longing for their respective homes, even though they might come from different places. The prominence of nostalgia, empathy, and kindness in *My Neighbor Totoro* makes a stark contrast to the bleak realism of *Grave of the Fireflies*, in which the dire circumstances of the war seem to have rendered adults powerless to rescue the siblings, even if they are empathetic to their plights. *Grave of the Fireflies* reminds us of the sad fate of many children who found themselves in extremely vulnerable positions during the war. *My Neighbor Totoro*, on the other hand, imagines a redemptive scenario in which children, nurtured and empowered by adults and nature surrounding them, overcome their struggles and challenges on their own.

A Snapshot from the Past

Miyazaki and Hisaishi portray this kind of nostalgia, something like a cross-generational empathy, in their last collaboration on the album, "A Small Photograph" (I-9). Miyazaki's poem depicts Satsuki and Mei's coming across an old picture of their mother as a child. The inquisitive eyes of the girls notice various small details in the picture. She is wearing a "sepia-toned straw hat" and carrying an "unfamiliar puppy." She stands next to a gate of the house where you can see the crepe myrtle casting a shadow. But above all, they notice the "shining dimples" in "their mother's cheeks" and "a bright smile" on her face. Looking at the picture, the girls feel an "unreachable longing for the nostalgic (*natsukashii*) summer day in the distance." As the girls make sense of what they see in front of their eyes, they understand that their mother, too, was once a young girl, with her own adventures and memories. The photograph, which seems to freeze in time a bright summer's day from the past, urges the girls to imagine their mother's personal history.

Hisaishi's music for the song resembles his other melodies that are "rich in nuance" and more reflective, such as "My Neighbor Totoro" and "Mother." Like many other songs on the album, "A Small Photograph" is in a simple verse-chorus form. A gentle introduction, featuring an acoustic guitar and flute against the soft accompaniment of a synthesizer and plucked string bass, starts the piece. The prominence of acoustic instruments, especially the delicate strums of the guitar, points to the style of Japanese popular folk music (*fōku songu*) that emerged in the 1960s (Stevens 2008, 44). The timbral quality of the song and its moderate tempo set the reflective mood of the song. The song starts and ends in the key of Db major, but throughout the verse and chorus, Hisaishi inserts chromatic chords in unexpected places to create a sense of instability that matches the bittersweet mood of Miyazaki's poem. As in "Mother" or "A Lost Child," the emotional intensity of the song rises in the chorus (0:55). The harmonic rhythm increases, propelling the melody forward (Example 17). The texture thickens in the chorus section with the addition of a percussion instrument, evocative of Hisaishi's "minimal and ethnic" style. Hisaishi also overdubs his own voice to harmonize with himself. The song ends with an upward gesture landing on a Db near the upper extreme of the range of the song.

Considering Miyazaki's adamant opposition to the widespread interpretation of *My Neighbor Totoro* as a "nostalgia piece," his use of the word "*natsukashii*" in this poem comes as a surprise. However, the nostalgia explored in this song differs from the self-indulgent form of yearning for the past that

O-ka - sa-n ga chi-i-sa-na o - n-na-no ko da - tta ko-ro no sha-shi - n

Example 17 *"A Small Photograph" (I-9, 0:55), the opening measures of the first chorus.*

Miyazaki problematizes. The poem has the children thinking about their mother's childhood. Because they do not have first-hand knowledge of their mother's lived experience, they are compelled to fill in the gap, using their own imagination and empathy. Miyazaki here characterizes the urge to engage in this mental process—the girls' desire to understand what the mother's childhood was like for her—as a form of nostalgia. This, perhaps, is what he means by the observation he made in his 1979 essay, "Nostalgia for a Lost World," that even very young children can experience nostalgia (Miyazaki 1996, 43).

Despite its poetic and musical appeal, Miyazaki and Hisaishi excluded "A Small Photograph," from the soundtrack of the film altogether. Fans of *My Neighbor Totoro* probably can also tell that no scene corresponding to the one described in Miyazaki's poem takes place in the film. Unlike other songs that relate to characters, objects, and dramatic situations as they appear in the film, the scene described in "A Small Photograph" seems to exist outside of the narrative.

Coming Home to Satsuki and Mei's House

On one clear brisk morning in late December 2018, I visited Satsuki and Mei's house, a life-sized model of the house from

My Neighbor Totoro. The building opened in 2005 during the World Expo just east of Nagoya, the third largest city in central Japan located between Tokyo and Osaka. Miyazaki Hayao's son Gorō oversaw the construction of the house (Miyazaki Gorō 2013, 209). Nearly fifteen years after the expo, the house continues to operate as a tourist destination for many fans of the film.

I was, however, not alone in this pilgrimage. For a few weeks, I had been visiting my family, who all happened to live in Nagoya, with my American husband. Hence, the trip to Satsuki and Mei's house turned out to be a large family outing involving my parents, my sister-in-law, my niece, my husband, and me. (My brother was at work and unable to join us.) We met at the subway station down the hill from my parents' apartment and took a series of public transportation, old and new, to the destination. These included a subway, a maglev train (which paled in comparison to the flying Catbus), and a bus, which took us to an empty spot within the desolate former site of the expo, now operating as a park. From there, we took a leisurely stroll through the empty park, passing by signs warning us of wild boars and a walled-off traditional Japanese villa facing the lake.

Once we had reached the welcome center and the appointed time for our visit had arrived, the guide, a middle-aged man, led us and several other visitors to Satsuki and Mei's house. In the film, the house embodies many of the dualities that occupied the film's creators such as nature and culture (the proximity of the structure to the surrounding forest), East and West (the eclectic style of the house that combines traditional Japanese and Western architectural elements), and life and death (the vitality of the sisters against the absence of their mother). From the entrance gate, I recognized the unique silhouette of the house. The red-roofed sunroom (the father's study) with pointy spindles seemed to jut out, in an awkward but also strangely harmonious way, from the otherwise traditional Japanese house.

The guide explained to us that the house was not exactly what we might have expected from the film. It represented how the family lived together *after* the mother's return from the hospital. We started by walking around the house, looking into the sunroom, moving to the veranda (*engawa*), and turning around the corner to the backdoor that leads to the kitchen. From the outside, the guide pointed out, the father had apparently tried to stabilize the precariously rotting trellis by wrapping some wires and stacking some bricks around one of the pillars. (One got the sense that he was, after all, an archaeologist and not an engineer.) As seen in the movie, there was a pump well with a broken bucket near the back door. On the ground, we noticed small tea sets and other toys scattered as if someone had been playing in the yard. The site was full of such small details that kept us marveling at the creators' attention to detail.

After looking around the house and taking some pictures, we moved inside where we met additional guides. We were told to wander freely around the house, open different doors and drawers, and look and touch objects. The guides told us that there were 5,000 items in this installation! The house was smaller than I had imagined it would be. It reminded me that the film had mostly been shot from the viewpoint of small children. Opening the drawers, my father and I marveled at the vintage toys, packaged foods, and other household items. I could not recognize many of the brands from the film or in real life, but seeing these objects in one place created a sense of timelessness. As I looked around, I also tried to remember scenes from the film—such as the march of the *susuwatari* across the ceiling—that took place inside the house.

At a certain point, I noticed my mother talking excitedly to a guide, a young woman perhaps in her twenties, in the bathroom. The site of the two circular bathtubs seemed to have suddenly brought back memories from her past, growing up near Nagoya in the 1950s. She was explaining that her family used to control the temperature of the bathwater by mixing water from two different tubs. From then on, everything about the house seemed to trigger a memory from her past. Seeing her interact with the surroundings this way made me realize that the visit to Satsuki and Mei's house was a very different experience for her. It also made me wonder what it must have been like for her to grow up in a house like that. What I experienced that day, of course, was an empathetic form of nostalgia that Miyazaki writes about in his poem "A Small Photograph."

* * *

Thinking about my mother's childhood home that day, in turn, made me think back to my own. While I spent my preadolescent years in Chiba, Japan, I was born and raised in Port Moresby, Papua New Guinea, in the South Pacific, separated by a distance of thousands of miles from the small village in Aichi Prefecture where my mother grew up. Although I did like to spend my free time reading indoors, my brother and I would often run around barefoot in the yard with our neighbors' kids. (To the embarrassment of our parents and consternation of people around us, the habit persisted for some time when we moved to Japan.) The hot tropical sun was always bright against the clear blue sky during the day, and the nights were filled with brilliant southern stars. Hibiscus flowers, bright red against the deep green leaves, bloomed only for a day and shriveled by the next morning. When the flowers were still in bloom, we would tear out the stamens, dotted with tiny balls of yellow pollens, and stick them into the small sand pits to fish out unsuspecting antlion larvae. Held between the fingers, the tiny but terrific-looking antlions always felt oddly squishy. After a while, we would let them wiggle back into their pits. Memories like these, fragmentary, vivid, and at the same time hazy, cycled through my mind that day.

More recently, as I walked through the wooded area of the university campus where I work, I remembered a tall cherry tree in front of the house where we used to live. The tree produced small red fruits that oozed grainy yellowish pulp with a coyly sweet smell when squeezed. The birds and bats seemed to like them, but they were not edible for humans (although I'm sure I must have tasted it at some point). I don't recall its limbs being thick and sturdy, like the camphor tree in *My Neighbor Totoro*. Instead, the tree had many skinny branches that made it easy for us to hook our hands and feet in order to climb higher. My mom would later tell me how she used to worry about us falling from the tree when she looked out the window and saw us dangling from the branches. Fortunately, we never did. Unlike Satsuki and Mei, my brother and I never met Totoro (or rather, I don't remember meeting Totoro) when we were growing up. Yet thinking back to my childhood, I cannot but wonder if some guardian spirit, a kind of tropical Totoro, had been watching over us. At night, if I strain my ears, I might still be able to hear Totoro's ocarina. I hope you can.

Notes

Introduction

1 One exception is Koizumi (2010). See Chapter 3 for more on a summary of her discussion on music and nostalgia.

2 An English translation of this essay is included in Miyazaki (2009, 350–77), with the title "*Totoro* Was Not Made as a Nostalgia Piece."

3 Dodd (2004, 14) argues that the nostalgic "mood" associated with *furusato* precedes the time Robertson studies, dating back to the eight-century anthology of poems *Man'yōshū*.

4 Article 9 of Japan's postwar constitution states that "the Japanese people forever renounces war as a sovereign right of the nation" and prohibits the state from maintaining armed forces intended to resolve international conflicts. For an English translation of the Constitution maintained on the website of the National Diet Library, see https://www.ndl.go.jp/constitution/e/etc/c01.html.

5 Robertson (1991) also discusses the tension between villagers and newly arrived transplants in Kodaira City, a formerly rural community in Western Tokyo, not far from Tokorozawa, the supposed setting of *My Neighbor Totoro*.

6 An English translation of this essay is included in Miyazaki (2009, 17–24). See also Cavallaro (2015, 30–31) for another interpretation of this essay.

Chapter 1

1   Biographies of Miyazaki in English include McCarthy (1999), Cavallaro (2015), Greenberg (2018), and Napier (2018). There are two collections of essays and other writings by Miyazaki (2009 and 2014) in English translations.

2   See also Roedder (2013) for more information about Hisaishi's biography.

3   Brummett (2014, ix) defines steampunk as "a new movement, largely aesthetic," emerging in the early 1990s that "resituates aesthetic elements from the Age of Steam into our world." Birmingham (2014, 65–66) notes the overlapping of steampunk aesthetics and anti-modern stance in Miyazaki's animated films.

4   Hisaishi's career has been marked by diverse creative outlets, ranging from esoteric concert music to commercial works. This diversity mirrors the artistic flexibility observed by Wade (2014, 9).

5   The two *kanji* (borrowed Chinese characters) that make up Hisaishi's name can be read alternatively as *ku-ishi* approximating the sound of "Quincy," pronounced as "kuinshī" in Japanese (Koizumi 2010, 61).

6   Smith's book on film soundtracks, *Sound of Commerce: Marketing Popular Film Music* (1998), provides an excellent study of industry practice in the United States.

7   According to Steinberg (2012, viii), the term "media mix" came into popular use in Japan in the late 1980s to describe "the cross-media serialization and circulation of entertainment franchises" but has its roots in the 1960s. According to Allison (2006, 9–10), this proliferation of products across various media makes it possible for Japanese products to "spread—and incite desires—across various surfaces, portals, and avenues for making and marketing fun." Drawing from Sigmund Freud, Allison describes this characteristic as "polymorphously perverse."

8 Incidentally, Hosono Haruomi, a member of Yellow Magic Orchestra, was one of the composers that Tokuma pushed but ultimately dropped from the project. Hosono did compose the song, "Nausicaä of the Valley of the Wind," based on lyrics by Matsumoto Takashi, which was used widely in the film's promotional campaign as its "symbol theme song." It was, however, not included on the soundtrack of the film itself (Kanō 2006, 61).

9 In US film industry practice, such meetings are called spotting sessions.

Chapter 2

1 For additional historical overviews of Meiji-Era music education in Japan, see Eppstein (1994) and Miller (2004).

2 *Archives of Studio Ghibli* (1996, 82) includes three drafts of the lyrics, one of which is in Miyazaki's own handwriting, that shows how the director and his creative team refined Miyazaki's ideas for the song by replacing words and phrases.

3 The descending third sequence, also known as descending 5–6 sequence, arranges a series of chords whose roots alternate between a descent by a fourth and an ascent by a step (for example, F—C—Dm—Am). Typically, Hisaishi alternates between root position and first inversion chords to create a bass line that moves stepwise (for example, F—C/E—Dm—Am/C). By chromatic harmonies, I refer to chords involving chromatically altered pitches that do not belong to the given scale of the piece (for example, C minor in the key of C Major). Extended chords refer to chords built on triads with added notes beyond the seventh.

4   Some *dōyō*, especially those composed by Yamada Kōsaku have meter changes to better reflect Japanese speech pattern (Manabe 2009, 179–86).

5   Hiragana and katakana are two of the three components of the Japanese writing system. Both are phonetic lettering systems comprised of vowels and consonant-vowel combinations. The third component is *kanji*, which are characters adopted from Chinese. Of the three, *hiragana* is the most fundamental system and is used in a variety of settings. The use of *katakana* is restricted, typically for transliterated foreign words and names or for loan words.

6   A whole-tone scale is a scale (pattern of notes) made up of a series of six notes that are a whole step away from each other. Both major and minor scales have a combination of whole and half steps. There are only two types of whole-tone scales: C–D–E–F♯–G♯–A♯–(C) and C♯–D♯–F–G–A–B–(C♯).

Chapter 3

1   In his 1998 monograph, *The Sounds of Commerce*, Smith makes a similar observation about Mancini's "Moon River" in *Breakfast at Tiffany's*, stating that the song and the title

tune "gave the score a sense of formal unity through their repetition" (80).

2 With its timbre in the synthesizer and its slowly unfolding play of textures, this cue is reminiscent of another from his film, *Nausicaä of the Valley of the Wind*, titled "In the Rotting Sea" (Fukai nite) on its soundtrack album (Hisaishi 1983). The music from the earlier film accompanies a parallel scene, in which the title character wakes up at the bottom of a toxic forest after an unexpected fall.

3 *Koinobori* are carp-shaped streamers flown on "Children's Day" (kodomo no hi), celebrated on May 5.

Chapter 4

1 Hisaishi typically transforms "The Path of the Wind" by changing the orchestration, keeping the melody of the song intact. He employs the same technique for "My Neighbor Totoro," but he also subjects it to motivic development, especially during Mei's chase for Small Totoro, when he extracts a small portion of the melody, the Totoro refrain, and changes its rhythm and pitches.

2 The melody starts with a series of ascending gestures featuring leaps that give the impression of a gapped scale such as the *niroku-nuki* pentatonic scale. However, the closing gesture of the initial phrase contains notes that are not part of the pentatonic scale. The contrasting middle section moves to A♭ major. Furthermore, the harmonic language of the song suggests interpretations of it in the keys of C minor and E♭ major. I thank Noriko Manabe, the series editor of 33 1/3 Japan, for this insight.

3 Morris-Suzuki (2013, 230) identifies a particular form of environmentalism in Japan called *airin shisō* that emerged in late Meiji and Taishō eras. She summarizes it as "an intriguing mixture of ecological science and nationalist romanticism."

Chapter 5

1 See Robertson (1988, 500–501) for a more thorough discussion of the long-standing association between mother and *furusato* [home].

Chapter 6

1 See also discussion of liminality in contemporary Japanese animation including Miyazaki's *Spirited Away* in Napier (2005, 171).

2 Miyazaki worked at Tōei Animation, which produced *Gegege no kitarō* between 1963 and 1971.

References

Allison, Anne (2006), *Millenial Monsters: Japanese Toys and the Global Imagination*, Berkeley: University of California Press.

Archives of Studio Ghibli (1996), vol. 2 *Tonari no Totoro / Hotaru no haka*, Tokyo: Tokuma Shoten.

Asano, Atsuko (2013), "Totoro no tonari de: shōjo no kaihō no monogatari," in *Tonari no Totoro*, Jiburi no kyōkasho 3, 8–22, Tokyo: Bungeishunjū.

Atkins, E. Taylor (2001), *Blue Nippon: Authenticating Jazz in Japan*, Durham, NC: Duke University Press.

Befu, Harumi (2001), *Hegemony of Homogeneity: An Anthropological Analysis of "Nihonjinron,"* Melbourne: Trans Pacific Press.

Bellano, Marco (2010), "The Parts and the Whole: Audiovisual Strategies in the Cinema of Hayao Miyazaki and Joe Hisaishi," *Animation Journal* 18 (2010): 4–54.

Bellano, Marco (2012), "From Albums to Images: Studio Ghibli's Image Albums and Their Impact on Audiovisual Strategies," *Trans-Revista Transcultural de Música/Transcultural Music Review* 16 https://www.sibetrans.com/trans/public/docs/trans_16_01.pdf.

Bender, Shawn Morgan (2012), *Taiko Boom: Japanese Drumming in Place and Motion*, Berkeley: University of California Press.

Birmingham, Elizabeth (2014), "Antimodernism as the Rhetoric of Steampunk Anime: *Fullmetal Alchemist*, Technological Anxieties, and Controlling the Machine," in *Clockwork Rhetoric: The Language and Style of Steampunk*, ed. Barry Brummett, 61–79, Jackson, University Press of Mississippi.

Bourdaghs, Michael K. (2012), *Sayonara Amerika, Sayonara Nippon: A Geopolitical Prehistory of J-Pop*, New York: Columbia University Press.

Boym, Svetlana (2001), *The Future of Nostalgia*, New York: Basic Books.

Brummett, Barry (2014), "Editor's Introduction: The Rhetoric of Steampunk," in *Clockwork Rhetoric: The Language and Style of Steampunk*, ed. Barry Brummett, ix–xiii, Jackson, University Press of Mississippi.

Cavallaro, Dani (2015), *Hayao Miyazaki's World Picture*, Jefferson, NC: McFarland.

Chion, Michel (1994), *Audio-Vision: Sound on Screen*, ed. and trans. Claudia Gorbman, New York: Columbia University Press.

Davis, Fred (1979), *Yearning for Yesterday: Nostalgia, Art, and Society*, New York: Free Press.

Dodd, Stephen (2004), *Writing Home: Representations of the Native Place in Modern Japanese Literature*, Cambridge, MA: Harvard University Press.

Eppstein, Ury (1994), *The Beginning of Western Music in Meiji Era Japan*, Lewiston, NY: Edwin Mellen Press.

Figal, Gerald (1999), *Civilization and Monsters: Spirits of Modernity in Meiji Japan*, Durham, NC: Duke University Press.

Foster, Michael Dylan (2015), *The Book of Yōkai: Mysterious Creatures of Japanese Folklore*, Berkeley: University of California Press.

Goldmark, Daniel (2005), *Tunes for 'Toons: Music and the Hollywood Cartoon*, Berkeley: University of California Press.

Greenberg, Raz (2018), *Hayao Miyazaki: Exploring the Early Work of Japan's Greatest Animator*, New York: Bloomsbury.

Hisaishi, Joe (1988), "Nihon ga butai demo aete sore o ishiki shinakatta," in *Jiburi roman arubamu: "Tonari no Totoro,"* 148–50, Tokyo: Tokuma Shoten.

Hisaishi, Joe (1992), *I Am: Haruka naru ongaku no michi e*, Tokyo: Media Fakutorī.

Hisaishi, Joe (2006), *Kandō o tsukure masuka?* Tokyo: Kadokawa Shoten.

Hisaishi, Joe (2007), *35mm nikki*, Tokyo: Takarajimasha.

Hisaishi, Joe (2014), *Piano kyokushū: "Tonari no Totoro,"* Tokyo: kmp.

Hughes, David W. (2008), *Traditional Folk Song in Modern Japan: Sources, Sentiment and Society*, Folkeston, UK: Global Oriental.

Ivy, Marilyn (1995), *Discourses of the Vanishing: Modernity, Phantasm, Japan*, Chicago: University of Chicago Press.

Kanō, Seiji (2006), *Miyazaki Hayao Zensho*, Tokyo: Firumu Āto Sha.

Key, Alexander (1970), The Incredible Tide, Philadelphia, Westminster Press.

Kihara, Hirokatsu (2018), *Futari no Totoro: Miyazaki Hayao to "Tonari no Totoro" no jidai*, Tokyo: Kōdansha.

Koizumi, Kyoko (2010), "An Animated Partnership: Joe Hisaishi's Musical Contributions to Hayao Miyazaki's Films," in *Drawn to Sound: Animation Film Music and Sonicity*, edited by Rebecca Coyle, 60–74, London: Equinox.

Manabe, Noriko (2009), "Western Music in Japan: The Evolution of Styles in Children's Songs, Hip-Hop, and Other Genres," PhD diss., City University of New York.

McCarthy, Helen (1999), *Hayao Miyazaki: Master of Japanese Animation: Films, Themes, Artistry*, Berkeley: Stone Bridge Press.

McDonald, Keiko I. (2006), *Reading a Japanese Film: Cinema in Context*, Honolulu: University of Hawai'i Press.

Miller, Richard C. (2004), "Music and Musicology in the Engineering of National Identity in Meiji Japan: Modernization Strategies of the Music Investigation Committee, 1870–1900," PhD diss., University of Wisconsin-Madison.

Miyazaki, Gorō (2013), "'Makkuro Kurosuke dete oide!' no ie," in *Tonari no Totoro*, Jiburi no kyōkasha 3, 209–215, Tokyo: Bungeishunjū.

Miyazaki, Hayao (1988), "Miyazaki Hayao intabyū: Totoro wa natsukashisa kara tsukutta sakuhin ja naindesu," in *Jiburi roman arubamu: "Tonari no Totoro,"* 122–39, Tokyo: Tokuma Shoten.

Miyazaki, Hayao (1996), *Shuppatsuten*, 1979–1996, Tokyo: Tokuma Shoten.

Miyazaki, Hayao (2005), *The Art of "My Neighbor Totoro,"* San Francisco: VIZ Media.

Miyazaki, Hayao (2009), *Starting Point, 1979–1996*, trans. Beth Cary and Frederik L. Schodt, San Francisco: VIZ Media.

Miyazaki, Hayao (2013), *Kaze no kaeru basho: Naushika kara Chihiro made no kiseki*, Tokyo: Bungeishunjū.

Miyazaki, Hayao (2014), *Turning Point, 1997–2008*, trans. Beth Cary and Frederik L. Schodt, San Francisco: VIZ Media.

Miyazaki, Hayao (2018), *Totoro no umareta tokoro*, Tokyo: Iwanami Shoten.

Miyazaki, Hayao and Nagakawa Rieko (1987), "Taidan Miyazaki Hayao vs Nakagawa Rieko: Koe o hariage, min'na de utaeru uta ga hoshii," *Animage*, June, 28–31.

Moriss-Suzuki, Tessa (2013), "The Nature of Empire: Forest Ecology, Colonialism and Survival Politics in Japan's Imperial Order," *Japanese Studies* 33, no. 3: 225–42.

Nakao, Sasuke (1966), *Nōkō no kigen to saibai shokubutsu*, Tokyo: Iwanami Shoten.

Napier, Susan (2005), *Anime from "Akira" to "Howl's Moving Castle": Experiencing Contemporary Japanese Animation*, updated edition, New York: St. Martin's Griffin.

Napier, Susan (2018), *Miyazakiworld: A Life in Art*, New Haven: Yale University Press.

Odell, Colin and Michelle Le Blanc (2015), *Studio Ghibli: The Films of Hayao Miyazaki and Isao Takahata*, Harpenden, UK: Kamera Brooks.

Papp, Zilia (2010), *Traditional Monster Imagery in Manga, Anima and Japanese Cinema*, Folkestone, UK: Global Oriental.

Robertson, Jennifer (1988), "*Furusato* Japan: The Culture and Politics of Nostalgia," *International Journal of Politics, Culture, and Society* 1, no. 4: 494–518.

Robertson, Jennifer (1991), *Native and Newcomer: Making and Remaking a Japanese City*, Berkeley: University of California Press.

Roedder, Alexandra Christina (2013), "'Japanamerica' or 'Amerijapan'? Globalization, Localization, and the Film Scoring Practices of Joe Hisaishi," PhD diss., UCLA.

Schodt, Frederik L (2012), *Manga! Manga! The World of Japanese Comics*, US edition, New York: Kodansha USA.

Schwartz, K. Robert (1996), *Minimalists*, London: Pahidon.

Shiba, Shigeharu (1988), "*Naushika Rapyuta* ijō ni shinkei o tsukatta tokoro mo," in *Jiburi roman arubamu: "Tonari no Totoro*," 146–47, Tokyo: Tokumashoten.

Smith, Jeff (1998), *The Sound of Commerce: Marketing Popular Film Music*, New York: Columbia University Press.

Starobinski, Jean (1966), "The Idea of Nostalgia," trans. William Kemp, *Diogenes* 14, no. 54 (June): 81–103.

Steinberg, Marc (2012), *Anime's Media Mix: Franchising Toys and Characters in Japan*, Minneapolis: University of Minnesota Press.

Sterling, Marvin D. (2010). *Babylon East: Performing Dancehall, Roots Reggae, and Rastafari in Japan*, Durham, NC: Duke University Press.

Stevens, Carolyn S. (2008), *Japanese Popular Music: Culture, Authenticity, and Power*, London: Routledge.

Suishō Takashi and Yamamoto Motoki (1987), "Rekōdo•rebyū,"
　　Animage, December: 198.

Suishō Takashi and Yamamoto Motoki (1988), "Rekōdo•rebyū,"
　　Animage, May: 190.

Suzuki, Toshio (2011), *Jiburi no tetsugaku: Kawaru mono to
　　kawaranai mono*, Tokyo: Iwanami Shoten.

Suzuki, Toshio (2013), "Nihon date sēsaku kara umareta kiseki,"
　　in *Tonari no Totoro*, Jiburi no kyōkasho 3, 39–45, Tokyo:
　　Bungeishunjū.

"Sutajio Jiburi monogatari: *Tonari no Totoro* hen" (2013), in *Tonari
　　no Totoro*, Jiburi no kyōkasho 3, 25–38, Tokyo: Bungeishunjū.

Swale, Alistair (2015), "Miyazaki Hayao and the Aesthetics of
　　Imagination: Nostalgia and Memory in *Sprited Away*," *Asian
　　Studies Review* 39, no. 3: 413–29.

Takahata, Isao (1991), *Eiga o tsukurinagara kangaeta koto*, Tokyo:
　　Tokuma Shoten.

Tannock, Stuart (1995), "Nostalgia Critique," *Cultural Studies* 9, no.
　　3: 453–64.

Thomas, Julia Adeney (2001), *Reconfiguring Modernity: Concepts
　　of Nature in Japanese Political Ideology*, Berkeley: University of
　　California Press.

Wade, Bonnie C. (2014), *Composing Japanese Musical Modernity*,
　　Chicago: University of Chicago Press.

Watanabe, Takashi ([1987] 2018), "*Tonari no Totoro* imēji songu
　　shū ni tsuite," liner notes to *Tonari no Totoro: Imēji songu shū*,
　　by Joe Hisaishi, Studio Ghibli Records, TIJA-10014, 33 1/3 rmp.

Wilson, Janelle L. (2014), *Nostalgia: Sanctuary of Meaning*, Duluth,
　　MN: Martin Library.

Yamasaki, Aki (2010), "*Cowboy Bebop*: Corporate Strategies for
　　Animation Music Products in Japan," in *Drawn to Sound
　　Drawn to Sound: Animation Film Music and Sonicity*, edited by
　　Rebecca Coyle, 209–22, London: Equinox.

Yamasaki, Aki (2014), "The Emergence of Singing Voice Actors/ Actresses: The Crossover Point of the Music Industry and the Animation Industry," in *Made in Japan: Studies in Popular Music*, ed. Tōru Mitsui, 191–207, New York: Routledge.

Yano, Christine R. (2002), *Tears of Longing: Nostalgia and the Nation in Japanese popular Song*, Cambridge: Harvard University Press.

Filmography

Buck, Chris and Jennifer Lee, dir. (2013), *Frozen*, Walt Disney Pictures.

Clements, Ron and John Musker, dir. (1988) *The Little Mermaid*, Walt Disney Pictures.

Clements, Ron and John Musker, dir. (1992), *Aladdin*, Walt Disney Pictures.

Yoshida, Shigetsugu et al., dir. (1974–1976), *Hajime ningen Gyātoruzu*, Tokyo Movie.

Edwards, Blake, dir. (1961), *Breakfast at Tiffany's*, Paramount Pictures.

Endō, Masaharu, Saitō Hiroshi, and Koshi Shigeo, dir. (1977), *Araiguma Rasukaru*, Nippon Animation.

Kuroda, Yoshio, dir. (1975), *Furandāsu no inu*, Nippon Animation.

Miyazaki, Hayao, dir. (1978), *Mirai shōnen Konan*, Nippon Animation.

Miyazaki, Hayao, dir. (1979), *Rupan Sansei: Kariosutoro no shiro*, Tokyo Movie.

Miyazaki, Hayao, dir. (1984), *Kaze no tani no Naushika*, Topcraft.

Miyazaki, Hayao, dir. (1986), *Tenkū no shiro Rapyuta*, Studio Ghibli.

Miyazaki, Hayao, dir. (1988), *My Neighbor Totoro*, Studio Ghibli.

Miyazaki, Hayao, dir. (1997), *Mononoke hime*, Studio Ghibli.

Miyazaki, Hayao, dir. (2001), *Sen to Chihiro no kamikakushi*, Studio Ghibli.

Miyazaki, Hayao, dir. (2008), *Gake no ue no Ponyo*, Studio Ghibli.

Miyazaki, Hayao, dir. (2013), *Kaze tachinu*, Studio Ghibli.

Takahata, Isao, dir. (1972), *Panda Kopanda*, Tokyo Movie.

Takahata, Isao, dir. (1973), *Panda Kopanda amefuri sākasu no maki*, Tokyo Movie.

Takahata, Isao, dir. (1974), *Arupusu no shōjo Haiji*, Zuiyō Eizō.

Takahata, Isao, dir. (1976), *Haha o tazunete sanzenri*, Nippon Animation.

Takahata, Isao, dir. (1979), *Akage no An*, Nippon Animation.

Takahata, Isao, dir. (1988), *Hotaru no haka*, Studio Ghibli.

Trousdale, Gary and Kirk Wise, dir. (1991), *Beauty and the Beast*, Walt Disney Pictures.

Yabushita, Taiji, dir. (1958), *Hakujaden*, Tōei Animation.

Discography

Eno, Brian (1978), *Ambien 1: Music for Airports*, Polydor, AMB 001, 33 1/3 rpm.

Hisaishi, Joe (1981), *Mkwaju*, Better Days, YF-7019-ND, 33 1/3 rpm.

Hisaishi, Joe (1982), *Information*, Japan Record, JAL-1005, 33 1/3 rpm.

Hisaishi, Joe (1985), *a•BET•City*, Japan Record, 28JAL–3016, 33 1/3 rpm.

Hisaishi, Joe (1987), "My Neighbor Totoro" / "Carrying You," Animage, 7AGS-12, 45 rpm.

Hisaishi, Joe (1987), *My Neighbor Totoro: Image Song Collection*, Animage, 25AGL–3053, 33 1/3 rpm.

Hisaishi, Joe (1987), *My Neighbor Totoro: Image Song Collection*, Animage, 25AGC–2053, Cassette.

Hisaishi, Joe (1987), *My Neighbor Totoro: Image Song Collection*, Animage, 32ATC–157, CD.

Hisaishi, Joe (1988), "My Neighbor Totoro" / "Hey Let's Go," Animage, 7AGS-14, 45 rpm.

Hisaishi, Joe (1988), "My Neighbor Totoro" / "Hey Let's Go," Animage, 10ATC-163, CD single.

Hisaishi, Joe (1988), *My Neighbor Totoro: Soundtrack Collection*, Animage, 25AGL–3058, 33 1/3 rpm.

Hisaishi, Joe (1988), *My Neighbor Totoro: Soundtrack Collection*, Animage, 25AGC–2058, Cassette.

Hisaishi, Joe (1988), *My Neighbor Totoro: Soundtrack Collection*, Animage, 32ATC–165, CD.

Hisaishi, Joe (1988), *My Neighbor Totoro: Mini Album*, Animage, 32ATC–165, CD.

Hisaishi, Joe (1988), *My Neighbor Totoro: Sound Book*, Animage, 25AGL–3062, 33 1/3 rpm.

Hisaishi, Joe (1988), *My Neighbor Totoro: Sound Book*, Animage, 25AGC–2062, Cassette.

Hisaishi, Joe (1988), *My Neighbor Totoro: Sound Book*, Animage, 32ATC–171, CD.

Hisaishi, Joe (1989), *My Neighbor Totoro: Drama Compilation*, Animage, 24ATC–174~5, CD.

Hisaishi, Joe (1990), *My Neighbor Totoro: High-Tech Series*, Animage, TKTA-20008, Cassette.

Hisaishi, Joe (1990), *My Neighbor Totoro: High-Tech Series*, Animage, TKCA-30014, CD.

Hisaishi, Joe (1992), *My Neighbor Totoro: Drama Compilation*, Animage, TKTA-20265, Cassette.

Hisaishi, Joe (1994), *My Neighbor Totoro Box*, Studio Ghibli Records TKCA-70340, CD.

Hisaishi, Joe (1996), *My Neighbor Totoro: Image Song Collection*, Studio Ghibli Records TKCA-71025, CD.

Hisaishi, Joe (1996), *My Neighbor Totoro: Soundtrack Collection*, Studio Ghibli Records TKCA-71026, CD.

Hisaishi, Joe (1996), *My Neighbor Totoro: Sound Book*, Studio Ghibli Records TKCA-71027, CD.

Hisaishi, Joe (1996), *My Neighbor Totoro: Drama Edition*, Studio Ghibli Records TKCA-71028, CD.

Hisaishi, Joe (1996), *My Neighbor Totoro: High-Tech Series*, Studio Ghibli Records TKCA-71029, CD.

Hisaishi, Joe (1999), *My Neighbor Totoro: Song & Karaoke*, Studio Ghibli Records TKCA-71780, CD.

Hisaishi, Joe (2000), "My Neighbor Totoro" / "Hey Let's Go," Studio Ghibli Records TKDA-71926, CD single.

Hisaishi, Joe (2002), *My Neighbor Totoro: Orchestra Series*, Studio Ghibli Records TKCA-72453, CD.

Hisaishi, Joe (2004), *My Neighbor Totoro: Image Song Collection*, Studio Ghibli Records TKCA-72724, CD.

Hisaishi, Joe (2004), *My Neighbor Totoro: Soundtrack Collection*, Studio Ghibli Records TKCA-72725, CD.

Hisaishi, Joe (2004), *My Neighbor Totoro: Sound Book*, Studio Ghibli Records TKCA-72726, CD.

Hisaishi, Joe (2004), *My Neighbor Totoro: High-Tech Series*, Studio Ghibli Records TKCA-72727, CD.

Hisaishi, Joe (2004), "My Neighbor Totoro" / "Hey Let's Go," Studio Ghibli Records TKCA-72756, CD single.

Hisaishi, Joe (2018), *My Neighbor Totoro: Image Song Collection*, Studio Ghibli Records TJJA-10014, 33 1/3 rpm.

Hisaishi, Joe (2018), *My Neighbor Totoro: Soundtrack Collection*, Studio Ghibli Records TJJA-10015, 33 1/3 rpm.

Hisaishi, Joe (2018), *My Neighbor Totoro: Sound Book*, Studio Ghibli Records TJJA-10016, 33 1/3 rpm.

Riley, Terry (1969), *Rainbow in Curved Air*, Columbia Masterworks, MS 7315, 33 1/3 rpm.

Track Lists

My Neighbor Totoro: Image Song Collection (**Animage Records 1987**)

	Title	Lyricist	Composer	Vocalist
1	My Neighbor Totoro	Miyazaki	Hisaishi	Inoue
2	The Path of the Wind	Miyazaki	Hisaishi	SCC*
3	Hey Let's Go	Nakagawa	Hisaishi	Inoue
4	A Lost Child	Nakagawa	Hisaishi	Inoue
5	Susuwatari	Nakagawa	Hisaishi	SSC
6	The Catbus	Nakagawa	Hisaishi	Kitahara
7	Fushigi Shiritori Song	Nakagawa	Hisaishi	Mori
8	Mother	Nakagawa	Hisaishi	Inoue
9	A Small Photograph	Miyazaki	Hisaishi	Hisaishi
10	Dondoko Festival	W. City	Hisaishi	Inoue
11	The Path of the Wind (instrumental)	N/A	Hisaishi	N/A

*Suginami Children's Chorus

My Neighbor Totoro: Soundtrack Collection (Anigame Records 1988)

	Title	Lyricist	Arranger	Vocalist
1	Hey Let's Go: Opening Theme Song	Nakagawa		Inoue
2	The Village in May		Hirabe	
3	A Haunted House			
4	Mei and the Susuwatari			
5	The Evening Wind			
6	I'm Not Scared			
7	Let's Go to the Hospital			
8	Mother			
9	The Little Monster			
10	Totoro		Hirabe (second half)	
11	A Huge Tree on the Tsukamori			
12	A Lost Child	Nakagawa		Inoue
13	The Path of the Wind			
14	A Soaking-Wet Monster			
15	Moonlit Flight		Hirabe (second half)	
16	Mei Is Missing			
17	The Catbus		Hirabe	
18	I'm So Glad		Hirabe	
19	My Neighbor Totoro: Ending Theme Song	Miyazaki		Inoue
20	Hey Let's Go (with chorus)	Nakagawa	Takeichi	Inoue, SCC

Index